SUCCESSFUL
—BIG—
BUSINESS
STRATEGIES
—FOR—
SMALL FIRMS

SUCCESSFUL
— BIG —
BUSINESS
STRATEGIES
— FOR —
SMALL FIRMS

*Modern management methods
which increase profitability*

Roger Bennett

KOGAN
PAGE

Acknowledgements

My thanks are due to Rosalind Bailey who word-processed the entire manuscript.

Copyright © Roger Bennett 1990

First published in Great Britain in 1990 by
Kogan Page Limited, 120 Pentonville Road,
London N1 9JN.

British Library Cataloguing in Publication Data
A CIP record for this book is available
from the British Library.

ISBN 0-7494-0236-9

Typeset by DP Photosetting, Aylesbury, Bucks
Printed and bound in Great Britain by
Biddles Limited, Guildford

Contents

1
Introduction

Franz Beckenbauer – manager of the West German football team and without doubt one of the most talented soccer players and managers in the history of the game – explained his success in the following manner.

'Football is an extremely uncomplicated activity. It has few rules, all of which are easy to understand and administer. Two teams play against each other for 90 minutes and both sides try to score as many goals as possible. Score more goals than the opposition and you win the contest. That's all there is to it.'

Business management, I suggest, is equally straightforward. You have revenues and costs and need to ensure that income exceeds expenditure by a generous margin. What could be less problematic?

Unfortunately, books about business management often overlook this plain and obvious reality. The discussion of business strategy and its implementation seems, alas, to have been shifted from the boardroom to the classroom! Yet, with the European Single Market only a year or so away, the critical examination of business strategy and tactics has *never* been so important.

Aims of the book

This book is intended to demystify some important aspects of business management, particularly as they relate to the determination of objectives and the evaluation of the adequacy of your company's existing policies for achieving targets. After reading the book you should be able to:

- define precisely and comprehensively the fundamental purpose of your firm;
- completely overhaul the procedures for deciding the business's strategies;
- relate chosen strategies to the implementation of policies;
- initiate a comprehensive do-it-yourself programme for auditing the effectiveness of your firm's strategies, tactics and operational systems.

How to use the text

The book contains numerous self-checks for you to answer in relation to your own company, plus lots of practical advice. This advice is, of course, subjective and might not be directly applicable to your particular business. Nevertheless, considering it should at least stimulate your thoughts about the topic discussed and force you to reappraise critically the usefulness of your company's current approaches to the issue.

People who actually run businesses (as opposed to the pundits who write and talk about them) are confronted by huge amounts of fragmented information. It is difficult (sometimes impossible) to see the wood for the trees because so many variables are potentially relevant to any business situation. Accordingly, straightforward step-by-step procedures are needed to help managers reduce the extent of the information they have to consider.

The aim is to resolve complex issues into a small handful of critical factors which reflect the fundamental *essence* of a problem and study only these key variables. Identification of the essential factors affecting the basic business functions (strategy formulation, organisation, procurement and marketing systems, etc) and the provision of fresh ideas for analysing them are among the core objectives of the book.

In the text you will find a list of ready-made criteria against which the efficiency of your business's current policies may be conveniently assessed. You will be invited to define:

- what precisely the firm exists to do;
- the characteristics and competencies that the business needs to possess in order to achieve its objectives;
- the adequacy of your firm's existing organisation structures.

My technique is simple and direct – all you need do to achieve success in relation to any and all of the problems I mention is adopt the following routine:

1. *Identify the dominant factors* affecting the situation. Establish what the issue is all about and the variables that will cause it to alter.
2. *List the available options*, making sure that *all* feasible possibilities are considered and not just some of them.
3. *Select the best solution*. This involves specifying appropriate criteria for deciding whether a particular outcome is to be regarded as a success or a failure.
4. *Describe the obstacles* that stand in the way of implementing chosen policies and how they will be surmounted.

Do this thoroughly for each of the subjects considered in the following chapters and you will develop a comprehensive and self-contained system for assessing the situation and operational performance of your firm. You should then be well positioned to revitalise the business.

Methodology of the approach

When asked to judge the usefulness of a physical object – a machine, a cutting instrument, or a piece of office equipment, for example – most people instinctively think first about its suitability for fulfilling the purpose for which it was originally intended. You ask, 'What function is the item supposed to perform?' and then 'How well does it complete that function?' A road map, for instance, is expected to show all the alternative routes available, the presence of major obstacles (road-works, rivers, unfinished bypasses, and so on), essential features of the local landscape (forests, lakes, estuaries), etc.

Business strategies and tactics should be looked at in a similar manner; they need to be instrumental and utilitarian – not works of art, and never works of fiction.

Need for practical methods

Each chapter explores a crucial aspect of business strategy and/or administration. Importantly, the book examines the *tactical and operational implications* of all the strategies discussed.

Some people may object to this on the grounds that strategy should be regarded as totally independent of tactics and operations. Personally, I see strategy, tactics and operations as *equally* important components of a unified whole; the best strategies in the world will fail if their operational requirements are shoddily implemented! Hence you will find much material on practical aspects of delegation, employee motivation, co-ordination of functions, interpersonal communications, etc, within the following pages.

What you will learn

Among the specific objectives of the text are that it should teach you:

- how to draft a statement of your company's mission;
- effective policies for controlling and motivating workers;
- how to lead the firm towards its objectives;
- the extent to which you should centralise the control of your business;
- how to improve morale and team spirit within the organisation;
- how to recognise your business's special competencies and potential.

Note that throughout the text I use the words firm, business, company and enterprise interchangeably, with no regard for any particular legal structure. The ideas and techniques discussed are (usually) applicable to any kind of organisation – public or private – whether it is a limited company, partnership or sole trader, although some will be of greater interest to larger firms than to very small businesses, and vice versa. Also, the word 'product' is used generically, meaning anything the firm has to sell and applying to services as well as physical goods.

2

How to Devise a Business Strategy

Introduction

This chapter seeks to help you to assess the adequacy of your business's present strategies. After reading the chapter you should be able to:

- think strategically;
- define the purpose of your firm;
- appreciate the need for diversification;
- relate strategies to tactics and day-to-day operations.

What strategy is

The *Concise Oxford Dictionary* defines 'strategy' in militaristic terms. Strategy, it asserts, is 'the imposition upon an enemy of a place and time and conditions for fighting preferred by oneself'. Business strategy may be similarly explained. It means choosing:

(a) a general direction for the firm;
(b) organisational structures; and
(c) policies and a style of management best suited to beating the competition.

Strategy and tactics

Strategy differs from 'tactics' in that whereas strategy involves the formulation of general, wide-ranging policies, tactics concern practical methods for implementing strategic decisions. Also, responsibility for tactics often lies with executives who are not themselves concerned with strategy determination. Examples of tactical management are decisions concerning:

- choice of an advertising agent;
- package design;
- use of outside consultants rather than internal staff to oversee projects;

- whether to operate on overdraft rather than (say) business development loans;
- selection of particular distributors;
- whether to purchase or lease company vehicles, or have them on contract hire with a repurchase option.

Strategies and plans

There are differences, moreover, between a strategy and a 'plan'. Strategies define the major overall goals of the organisation. Plans state how these goals are to be accomplished. Strategy concerns ideas, creativity and grand conceptions; plans are to do with mundane and instrumental measures for the efficient allocation of human, material, financial and other resources within the business.

Plans convert into tactics and hence into operations (eg, the organisation of work, allocation of duties, acquisition and deployment of assets, installation of feedback and appraisal systems, etc) for their implementation.

—————————————— *Checkpoint* ——————————————

How many days during the last six months have you and your senior colleagues spent on:

- resolving production and distribution difficulties;
- negotiating and overseeing budgets;
- planning the long term development of the company?

Which of these activities was the most important?

Examples of strategic decisions

Effective strategies cause the firm to offer the right products to the right markets at the right time and at the right quality and price. Examples of strategic decisions are:

- the products the firm will supply;
- which markets (foreign as well as domestic) to serve;
- quality and price levels;
- organisation structures and legal forms (public company, private company, how many departments and divisions within the business);
- how many workers to employ;
- whether to recognise trade unions and how, in general terms, employees are to be treated;
- how to finance the business (shares, loans, debentures, etc);
- whether to franchise retail outlets;
- branding strategies and the degree of product standardisation.

―――――――――――――― *Checkpoint* ――――――――――――――

Consider a date three or four years in the future. What is the *ideal* situation you would like your business to be in by that time?

● What have you done during the last six months to help to achieve this ideal situation?
● What barriers might prevent you attaining the ideal situation?

Why have a strategy

Some businesses do not bother formulating strategies, preferring instead to *respond* to situations, opportunistically, as they arise. Several (valid) reasons might be advanced for this: inaccuracy of forecasts, sudden and unforeseeable changes in laws, regulations and technical and market environments, the costs and inconveniences of long-range planning, etc. Moreover, many firms fail to consider strategy issues seriously until they are forced to do so following some catastrophic event (eg, loss of a crucial contract, collapse of an expensive project, inability to match a leading competitor's prices or quality levels) which dramatically exposes the inadequacy of their strategic planning systems. Such businesses then rush to establish strategies, discovering too late the gravity of their situations and the fact that different senior managers and departments see the firm's base objectives in entirely different ways.

Advantages of having strategies
The systematic formulation of strategies has many advantages.

1. The business is compelled to examine in fine detail its strengths and weaknesses and to explore its environments for opportunities and threats. This process itself generates useful information immediately applicable to day-to-day operations.
2. Strategies provide firm criteria against which the company's general progress may be assessed.
3. Important decisions are taken only after considering all the facts and available options, not in chaotic short-run crisis situations.
4. Long-term investments are properly evaluated.
5. The firm is ready to respond to predictable changes in consumer tastes and spending patterns.
6. Reactions to changes in competitors' behaviour may be decided in advance.
7. Speculation about possible future events and circumstances may cause the firm to discover ways of influencing the future for its own benefit.
8. The existence of a strategy provides a focal point towards which all the company's energies may be directed.

9. Co-ordination between subsidiaries, divisions and other component parts of the organisation is enhanced.
10. From 31 December 1992, UK firms must compete equally with all
European Community businesses. Not only should UK firms
devise strategies for fighting off European competitors here in
Britain, but they need also to discover fresh ways of promoting and
distributing their own products in the community at large.

Checkpoint

Imagine you are a reporter for the financial column of a leading
national newspaper and that your assignment for today is to cover the
county court bankruptcy/liquidation proceedings of your business.
What are the major causes of its failure and how will you describe
these to the outside world? For instance, would you attribute the
firm's collapse to incompetence among its senior employees, or to
objective circumstances beyond their control?

Strategy formulation

Conventional approaches to devising strategies suggest (rightly) that
every business should ask itself three basic questions, the answers to
which should provide a blueprint for the strategic development of the
firm. The three questions are as follows.

What business are we in?

Failure to define a business's range of interests sufficiently widely
makes it vulnerable to predatory competitors and to the adverse effects
of technical change. All the company's eggs are in just one or two
baskets so that technological obsolescence of a product or a successful
attack by a competing firm (price cuts, introduction of a new model, a
shift in customers' perceptions of the value and quality of the
competitor's output) may create enormous difficulties for the supplying
firm.

To illustrate this, consider the changeover from conventional
typewriting to word processing. Firms producing ordinary typewriters
were – in a limited sense – in the same industry as the manufacturers of
WPs (ie, the creation of letters, memoranda, reports and other 'hard
copy' documents), but employees' skills and their processes of manufacture had an essentially 'mechanical' orientation. They made and
assembled typing keys, carriages, roller bars, etc, and were not in a
position to transfer these (engineering) competencies to the computer-
based technologies that word processing involves (microelectronics,
computer programming, software design, and so on). Even the

materials from which WPs are constructed (circuit boards, microchips, plastic keyboards) are different from those in a typewriter.

Equally, consider a stationery firm. Is it in the paper business, or graphic design, or business communication generally? A stationer who concludes that the firm is in the wider office communications business and not concerned merely with the purchase, processing and resale of paper will be interested in *all* aspects of office communications and related equipment – photocopying methods and systems, telephone equipment, electronic mail, electronic diaries, relevant computer software, dictating machines – indeed anything to do with office communications. The product range of this firm will differ markedly from that of a stationer who simply designs letterheads and prints and sells commercial paper.

Checkpoint

Draw up a list of goals you would like the company to achieve (1) one year, (2) three years from now in each of the following areas:

— your market position *vis-à-vis* competitors;
— the firm's assets (fixed assets plus working capital);
— rates of return;
— major shifts in the structure of the firm's costs and revenues.

Which of your objectives are most important and why? Are the critical objectives receiving top priority?

What are the probabilities of your achieving each of the goals specified?

Answering the seemingly innocuous question 'What business are we in?' provides many useful insights into a company's susceptibility to external change and may suggest new activities it might profitably undertake. The aim is to relate the business's strengths to what it actually does – to dovetail its abilities and resources into the most lucrative market opportunities available and to identify profitable alternative and collateral activities.

Checkpoint

If yours is a single product business, how sensitive are its sales to changes in fashion, reduced consumer incomes or sudden increases in raw materials and other input prices?

Adviceline

Strategies that depend on a single product can be extremely problematic: random fluctuations in demand may disrupt production, and the firm's organisation and distribution systems become rigid in form. Your plant and equipment become increasingly specialised and thus cannot be used for other purposes when business is slack. Staff become unable or unwilling to undertake duties not strictly related to the single product.

Some degree of diversification is always useful. Its advantages include:

— spreading risk across several activities;
— being able to offer different credit terms for different products to different classes of consumer (hence balancing cash inflows among several markets and customer types);
— the creation of opportunities of introducing new selling and distribution methods (direct mail, franchising, cash and carry, and so on).

What business should we be in?

Firms sometimes become locked into a particular type of business without realising that alternative and more lucrative possibilities exist.

Checkpoint

• How do you expect each of your firm's current and intended markets to develop over the next three to five years? For each market, identify trends in:

— income;
— average age of consumers;
— consumer lifestyles.

• Have your competitors diversified into ancillary fields? If so, why?

You must examine carefully the profitabilities of various market segments and their potential for further expansion. Look also at the ease with which new markets may be entered. Now list – honestly and comprehensively – your firm's particular strengths and weaknesses as they relate to each actual and possible new market. Are you in fit shape to tackle the best of the available market opportunities? If not why not, and what must be done to remedy the situation?

Checkpoint

Strategies have lives analogous to those of people. They are conceived, they develop, mature and eventually die. The major difference is that, unlike humans, strategies can and should be quickly killed off as soon as they have outlived their usefulness.

On a piece of paper draw two lines. The first should be straight, as follows:

The far left of the line represents the day the organisation came into being, the far right shows when it will cease to exist. On this line, place a cross to indicate how far into its life you believe the organisation has progressed, given its current strategies. Justify your assessment.

The second line should be drawn similar to the one illustrated below. Peaks and troughs correspond to successes and failures, high spots and low spots in the organisation's history.

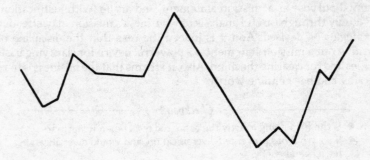

Looking back, were the troughs foreseeable and how might they have been avoided?

What do we have to do to get to where we want to be?
Clearly, the business needs to be headed towards the most attractive activities and market sectors. It should seek to operate anywhere it has a competitive advantage. Strategies for achieving this might involve:

- finding new ways of using existing capital and other resources;
- switching the market position (see below) of the firm's output, eg, from a low-price bottom end of the market location to a top-end high price sector of the same market;
- product and market diversification;
- structural reorganisation (see Chapter 4);

- capital investment;
- altering the financial structure of the business (eg, moving from debt to equity financing, entering or leaving the Unlisted Securities Market, etc).

Creating a strategy

There are five steps to creating and implementing a strategy. First, you need to define precisely the purpose of your business; then you must analyse its strengths and weaknesses, identify external constraints, determine particular strategic objectives, and execute the programme.

The purpose of the firm

Why was this business established in the first instance? What *exactly* does the organisation exist to do? Answer these questions honestly and you are three-quarters of the way towards discovering the true purpose of the firm.

American strategists refer to the declaration of a company's fundamental purpose as a 'mission statement' and argue (with justification) that only through careful analysis of a business's mission may effective strategies be devised. And it is indeed the case that the discipline of writing out a mission statement is a powerful device for clarifying basic issues and for clearing the mind. Also, it affirms that the business is here to stay and has genuine worth.

Checkpoint

- Is the firm doing exactly the same today as when it started?
- If so, what has prevented diversification, and would diversification have been beneficial?
- If not, what caused the changes – were they inevitable or were they implemented by choice?
- What would have happened if change had not occurred?

Mission statements

A mission statement is an outline of the firm's strategies at the highest level of generality – how it sees itself and what it wishes to achieve. To draft a mission statement for your company you must first determine each of the following issues:

- The scope of the firm's operations and the markets it wishes to serve (geographical, customer type, mail order versus retail outlet, etc).
- Desired market share and whether the firm intends leading or following its competitors.

- The degree of excellence to which the business aspires, including product quality levels, extent of customer care, staff development, etc.
- Whether the organisation will seek consciously to be a good employer and neighbour (and spend the money necessary for this), will not pollute the environment, and will always act in a socially responsible way.
- Whether the business is to operate at the top or bottom ends of its markets.
- The frequency with which new products and variations on existing models will be introduced.
- How the firm perceives the balance between the requirements of customers (price and quality policies), shareholders (dividend and profit retention policies) and employees (wages and working conditions).

When considering your business's mission you need to adopt a sober, mature and reflective outlook, bearing in mind:

— the age and calibre of the firm's plant and equipment;
— constraints on the feasibilities of major objectives;
— the successes and failures of other businesses with similar goals;
— how quickly the firm's environmental circumstances might change (missions are long-term commitments and should not be frequently revised, though they must never be allowed to become irrelevant or outdated).

Other factors to take into account are:

1. the business's history and traditions (eg, a firm with an established reputation for high quality – albeit expensive – output would not benefit from entering the trash end of a market even if that segment offered extremely profitable opportunities);
2. its strengths and competencies (see page 23); and
3. the extent of its resources. These include financial resources (such as cash reserves), the skills of employees, productive capacity and efficiency, control over inputs and access to channels of distribution.

Sample extracts from company mission statements

Mission statements should succinctly sum up the purpose and major intentions (to customers, shareholders, suppliers and employees) of the enterprise. The mission statement of a particular firm will contain much technical, product, market and other information and may occupy several pages. However, here are some brief extracts from actual mission statements to illustrate the idea.

- Our mission (Ford Motor Company) is to be the worldwide leader in automotive and auto-related products and services as well as in newer industries such as aerospace, communications and financial services.
- This business will produce and sell low-cost, functional lighting systems to UK television studios and will install these whenever required.
- This company seeks to be the market leader in the passenger car entertainment business and will achieve this through the frequent introduction of new models of high-quality, top-end-of-the-market car radios, speakers, cassette players and related equipment.
- Our mission is to search for oil and produce, refine and market petroleum and petroleum products throughout the world (multinational oil company).
- The firm will operate in the following markets: building and construction, transport, electrical machinery, and containers and packaging.
- We shall locate our subsidiaries where there are tax advantages and low energy costs.
- Our mission is to be a major factor in the worldwide movement of information (US telephone company).
- Our product range will comprise alloy piping, plate products, fabricated coil and seamless extrusions.
- To achieve customer satisfaction, the quality of our products and services must be paramount.
- We shall treat our employees with trust and respect.
- We shall provide an environment in which all staff can develop and advance on merit as far as their skills and talents will take them.
- The scope of this company's output will be restricted to power conversion equipment, information display, and power transmission equipment for the automotive and aircraft industries in Britain, Europe and the United States.
- Our purpose is to search continuously for fresh opportunities for developing measurement control technology and constantly to improve the quality and reliability of our products.
- We seek to provide shareholders with a financial return well above the average for our industry and to maintain the stability and security of their investments.
- All internal growth is to be financed from earnings.
- We shall aim not only to supply reliable products but also to provide a comprehensive after-sales service and facilities for customer care. This means a no-quibble refund for dissatisfied customers and continual effort to understand and meet our customers' needs.

- Our aim is to provide all employees with total security of tenure, training and development and above average remuneration, regardless of race, colour or sex.
- We shall seek to understand the difficulties that confront our suppliers, the constraints they face, and will co-operate with them in helping to achieve their quality improvement goals.

Who should determine the business's mission?

Everyone who works for the enterprise should support its mission. In practice, however, different managers may interpret the business's mission in entirely different ways. Thus it is essential that the mission statement is precise, explicit, neither too broad nor too narrow, and written in language that all interested employees can understand.

Checkpoint

By now you should be able to attempt an outline mission statement for your company. If you find this easy you are probably doing it incorrectly! Much careful thought is needed – defining a company's mission is more demanding than it first appears.

The first draft of the document might be formulated by a single person (eg, the chief executive or owner of the firm) and distributed for comment prior to general release, or by a committee specially convened for the task.

Committees may bring greater knowledge and a wider breadth of experience to strategy determination; equally they may not. And decision taking through committees can be extremely quarrelsome and slow. It is better, I suggest, to have just one or two people initially involved and follow up their proposals with a general meeting to discuss their recommendations. I say this for several reasons.

(a) Busy middle-rank executives are frequently short of time and not really interested in strategy issues. There is always some problem or other demanding their urgent attention, and these operational matters tend to monopolise their thoughts.
(b) Troublesome status differentials can arise between the managers invited to participate in strategy formulation and those left out.
(c) Top-class line managers are not necessarily good strategists.
(d) It is usually easier for one person to choose appropriate wording for the paragraphs that make up a mission statement than for statements to be collectively worded by a committee. Where committees are used it is common for the committee secretary actually to write the document; so why not have the initial draft prepared by a single person in the first place?
(e) A strategy committee could develop a reputation within the organisation of comprising ineffective senior managers who have

so little to do with their time that they fill out their working day by attending non-essential meetings of strategy committees.

(f) A single committee member might so confuse essentially straight-forward issues that missions and strategies are never actually determined.

(g) There is no clear-cut criterion to determine how often a strategy committee should meet. In consequence they might meet too frequently, causing great expense to the organisation (bearing in mind that participants will be highly paid executives whose time could be profitably spent elsewhere).

However it is done, it is vital that the people responsible for strategy matters are clearly identified. Too often, strategy is in fact determined in someone's head with little or no subsequent documentation. This creates continuity as well as communications difficulties: excellent strategies may be lost for ever if a key person leaves the firm.

Checkpoint

- If your company has a strategy committee, are its meetings effective?
- Does each session have an identifiable purpose?
- On average, how many useful ideas are contributed by each participant?
- If the number of people attending were reduced by one-third, what difference would this make to outcomes?

Adviceline

Having too many people on committees is a sure sign that employees within the organisation have insufficient work. It means that people are filling out their time attending non-essential meetings (see page 41). Anyone who fails to make significant comments during strategy (or indeed any other) meetings should be dropped and their efforts devoted to alternative tasks.

Appraising internal weaknesses and strengths

Checkpoint

List your firm's three major weaknesses and specify:

- their causes;
- what actions the firm can initiate in order to remedy them;
- any outside bodies (consultancies, banks, trade associations, etc) that might help you to deal with deficiencies.

What personal shortcomings in the senior management team might prevent your firm remedying its weaknesses?

Now read on and return to your list when you have completed the next section.

Strengths and weaknesses exist *within* the organisation; opportunities and threats (see below) normally originate outside. Strengths and weaknesses can relate to:

- customer care
- production efficiency
- staff resources and skills
- delivery periods
- ability to introduce new products and working methods
- ability to raise funds
- supply of components and materials inputs
- plant, equipment and vehicles
- flow of work between departments
- suitability of premises
- stock control
- product attractiveness
- quality control
- internal communications
- warehousing
- packaging and transport
- distribution arrangements
- availability of useful management information
- advertising and sales promotions
- dealership and discount systems.

How do the strengths and weaknesses of your company compare with those of leading competitors? Your task is to build on your strengths and overcome deficiencies.

Examine the firm's environments
Several external environments affect a business's operations. The most important of these are as follows.

The legal environment
The company needs a system for keeping abreast of parliamentary and other legislation affecting its work. Examples of laws that are crucially important for business are the 1987 Consumer Protection Act (which greatly increased a firm's liability for defective products), the 1978 Employment Protection Act (which defines the circumstances in which employees may be 'fairly' dismissed) and the 1985 amendments to the Equal Pay Act, which overnight rendered unlawful the job evaluation and staff grading schemes of many businesses.

Adviceline

At least one senior employee should be made responsible for monitoring changes in the firm's legal environment. Information on current and intended legislation is available through the magazines of trade and professional bodies, through *CBI News* and similar publications. Also there exist specialist information gathering organisations (Croner's, for example) which continuously update their legal databases and distribute details of new developments to their subscribers on a monthly basis.

Market environments

The company should constantly search for fresh market opportunities and for early warnings of decline in existing markets.

──────────────── *Checkpoint* ────────────────

- What criteria do you apply to the evaluation of market opportunities?
- How do you define an 'attractive' market?
- How frequently do you reassess the value of the company's markets?

Now read on and come back to these questions when you have completed the next section.

Attractive markets. Attractive markets have the following characteristics:

- They are large and expanding, with lots of new consumers coming on to the market as well as existing consumers buying more of the goods.
- Long run demand is reasonably assured.
- Your firm can increase or decrease its share of the market as it wishes (via price changes and variations in advertising and promotional activity) without triggering immediate responses from competitors.
- Unit profits are high and secure (note how market growth and profitability need not be coincidental).
- Revenues from selling to the market arrive continuously. There are few interruptions to cash flows.
- Outside firms find it difficult to enter the market (through lack of know-how, limited access to distribution outlets, etc).
- Consumer tastes and buying patterns are stable.
- The item is easy to produce, and production and distribution methods are not liable to unpredictable and uncontrollable change.
- Demand is reasonably constant.

Danger signals. Beware of the following situations:

- Holding a large share of a stagnant or declining market.
- Ill-considered entry into a new market (albeit a buoyant one) that requires technical, distribution and other skills that your business does not currently possess.
- The likelihood of new and aggressive competition from predatory new entrants to the market.
- Unpredictable technical change that could cause the obsolescence of the company's products.

The ideal situation is to have a high market share of an expanding and otherwise attractive market. Activities in declining and unprofitable markets should be replaced by more lucrative or promising operations.

You also need a suitable balance of products. Aim to have one or more safe and steady products that can be relied upon to generate a consistent cash flow, plus developing products with rapidly increasing market shares, and perhaps a few risky products which offer, nevertheless, the possibility of high financial returns.

─────────────────── *Checkpoint* ───────────────────

Are your business's percentage market shares of each of its key markets the same today as they were (1) a year ago, (2) three years ago? If not, how do you explain the changes that have occurred? Are the differences the consequence of strategic decisions taken by your company?

The competitive environment

Here you must examine the make-up and behaviour of competing businesses, their strengths and weaknesses, their product quality, efficiency, distribution methods, etc. Look particularly at their pricing policies and whether they are carrying substantial amounts of spare capacity (sudden price cuts are likely if this is the case). How quickly and easily can they introduce new products and, if they do, how quickly will you know about this? Ask yourself the following questions in relation to each major competitor.

- Are its marketing arrangements better than your own and, if so, what must you do to match the competitor in the marketing field?
- If the competitor has wide-ranging interests, has the experience it has acquired in other areas given it a competitive edge? What lessons can you draw from the competitor's diversification policy?
- Is the competitor likely to acquire other businesses in order to improve its competitive strength? If so, what are the market share and other implications for your company?
- Do you think the competitor is satisfied with its current market position, or will it want to expand its market share? How well

equipped is the competitor for achieving an increase in sales?
- In which market segments is the competitor most vulnerable to attack? How do you explain the competitor's vulnerabilities?
- Which of your possible marketing activities (a price cut, increase in advertising, etc) is most likely to provoke a hostile reaction from the competing firm? Why is this the case?

--------------------- *Checkpoint* ---------------------

Prepare a list of all the factors that might prevent your most dangerous competitor withdrawing from an important market. The list might include items such as: having to write off expensive equipment, loss of goodwill with distributors, desire to protect employees' jobs, loss of prestige, etc.

The competitive position of the business. This depends on your market share, product quality, marketing arrangements, on how consumers perceive your output and on your ability to alter products and/or the scale of operations at short notice.* Other relevant factors are as follows:

(a) How your cost structure compares with those of competing firms – including administrative and marketing costs as well as the costs of production.
(b) How easily you can make your firm's output appear different from and superior to that of other businesses.
(c) Your ability to operate in market niches not serviced by competing firms.
(d) Whether new entrants to your major markets would have to spend large amounts on setting up production, establishing brand images, obtaining access to distribution channels, etc.
(e) Your vulnerability to the loss of a small number of extremely large customers.
(f) The extent of your company's reliance on a handful of suppliers of materials, components and other inputs.

--------------------- *Checkpoint* ---------------------

Assess your firm's competitive position in relation to each of the above-mentioned six points.

The position of your product. The term 'market position' refers to how a product is perceived and rated by consumers in comparison with the products of competing firms.

See M E Porter, *Competitive Strategy*, Collier Macmillan 1981.

—————————— *Checkpoint* ——————————

How do you think the typical customer regards your output *vis-à-vis* those of competing companies in relation to each of the following:

● value for money;
● after-sales service;
● quality?

In a sense a product's position is its 'personality', as seen by the consumer. And it is possible to shift a product's position in a consumer's mind through modifying its characteristics, by advertising, public relations and other promotional activities. Consider any one of your company's products. Do consumers regard it as high-price high-quality; low-price, low-quality; low-price high-quality (Amstrad computers are a good example of this market position) or low-quality high-price? What aspects of the product and its presentation *cause* consumers to think in these terms?

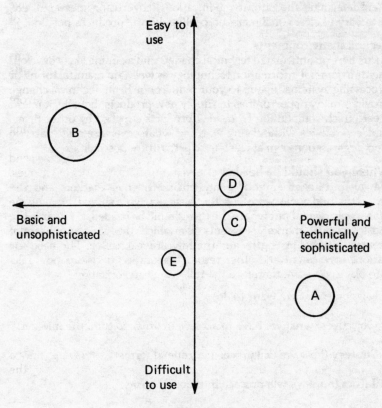

Figure 2.1

─────────────────── *Checkpoint* ───────────────────

Examine some other pairs of product characteristics – apart from quality and price – that are especially relevant to the product under consideration. Examples are: utility and design; speed and ease of operation; attractiveness of package and volume of package contents, etc.

Now compare the product with those of major competitors in relation to each pair of criteria. You could do this with a diagram as illustrated in Figure 2.1 on page 27. This shows the market position of a certain make of desk-top computer (as revealed by a survey of customer opinion) using the variables 'ease of use' on one axis and 'power and technical sophistication' on the other. The make in question is labelled 'A'. Other makes are denoted by letters B to E. Circle sizes are drawn roughly proportional to the estimated sales volume of each competing make.

You must select the *ideal* position for the product (the top right corner of the upper right-hand quadrant for the computer example above) and then determine the output modifications, advertising messages, etc, necessary to alter consumers' perceptions of the product's position.

Technical environments
Focus here on anticipated technical change, and examine likely developments in general information technology as well as in manufacturing or processing systems unique to your industry or firm. Technical change provides many opportunities to supply new products. Equally, it might create fresh competition from new products supplied by other firms. Sudden changes without any warning whatsoever are quite rare, so alert organisations can at least anticipate future possibilities.

Where you should be headed
Having put together your analyses of attractive markets and the strengths and weaknesses of the business, you should by now be reasonably clear about where the firm should be headed, ie towards the most lucrative market segments for which the company has the greatest internal strengths and the fewest weaknesses. The need for various investment and other resource allocation decisions now falls into place. We have therefore the following categorisation.

Mission (what we want to do)
↓
Objectives (what we have to achieve in order to fulfil the mission)
↓
Strategy (how we will proceed in general terms)
↓
Tactics (how we will proceed in practical terms)
↓
Operations (doing the work)

To illustrate, part of the mission of an electronic components manufacturer might be to dominate a certain automotive electronic component market within five years. In order to fulfil its mission it must achieve the objectives (among other things) of capturing a one-third share of a certain market segment within the next 12 months and introducing two new products. The company's strategies for meeting these objectives may include low prices, low profit mark-ups, generous discounts and exclusive dealership arrangements. Also, expenditure on research and development and trade magazine advertising will have to be greatly increased to facilitate the introduction of the new products.

Tactics revolve around the selection of particular dealers, choice of advertising media, a deliberate diminution in product quality in order to cut costs, use of a greater proportion of cheap and unskilled casual labour than in the past, etc. This is, of course, an enormous simplification of the strategy issues facing such a company, but it gives you the idea of what is involved.

Specification of objectives

An objective is a statement of something the business needs to accomplish in order to achieve its mission. The more concrete the company's mission statement, the easier it is to determine strategic objectives, since the mission statement (which represents in effect a 'constitution' for the business) imposes constraints on policies and generally defines the parameters of the strategies the company may pursue. Typically, objectives relate to such matters as financial returns, rates of growth, market shares, introduction of new products, efficiency improvements, cost cutting programmes, removal of competitors, and so on.

Rules for setting objectives

The following rules should be observed when setting objectives.

1. Objectives should be consistent. For example, the maximisation of short-term returns usually implies frequently switching from one market or line of activity to another, and would not be consistent with an objective of attaining long-term security and steady growth.
2. Objectives should follow a hierarchy, with the most general at the top and the most detailed and specific at the bottom.
3. Each objective should be accompanied by statements of:
   — who is responsible for its attainment;
   — when the objective is to be achieved;
   — how the objective is to be accomplished, including a specification of the resources necessary and where and how they will be acquired.
4. All objectives should relate directly and identifiably to the mission of the business.

5. Criteria for deciding whether an objective has been achieved should be predetermined.
6. Wherever possible, objectives should be stated in quantitative terms and, where extensive written instructions are required, should be written in simple English.

--- *Checkpoint* ---

How sensitive are your company's present objectives to technical change? Must they all be abandoned if manufacturing or other technologies suddenly alter? If this is the case, prepare a set of alternative objectives, each relating to a particular foreseeable technical situation.

Spirals of objectives

Objective setting should be an on-going process. Once a particular target has been achieved its effects and implications should be evaluated and new and more demanding objectives imposed. This will systematically stretch your firm's capabilities and lead to continuously improving performance in the longer run. Note, however, that targets should not be increased arbitrarily and/or in too short a period (see Chapter 6).

Adviceline

In devising objectives it is helpful to ask yourself the following questions.

- How does the firm's output differ from those of competitors and what should it do to take full advantage of these differences?
- Is the company's access to essential inputs (materials, labour, etc) assured and, if not, what must be done to guarantee continuity of supply?
- What additional resources are needed to improve the business's performance and where can these be found?
- How exactly will each proposed objective assist in beating the competition?

Implementation of strategy

The final step is to evaluate the organisation's ability to implement chosen strategies and to initiate measures for overcoming deficiencies. To do this you need to investigate the following questions:

(a) Are the firm's management information systems, forecasting procedures, means of co-ordinating activity, and general administration capable of supporting the policies needed to implement chosen plans, and if not why not?

(b) How adequate is the company's marketing and product research for specified tasks?
(c) Does the firm possess a reliable materials procurement system?
(d) What measures exist for ascertaining when existing products have reached the ends of their life cycles?
(e) Has the firm an organisation development programme capable of effecting structural change and, if so, how long will it take to implement structural alterations?
(f) What mechanisms exist for controlling expenditure?

The marketing potential of the business needs to be examined in relation to product, price, promotional and distribution policies. Products must be scrutinised *vis-à-vis* their consumer appeal, production cost and quality (decisions to vary the quality of output have many strategic implications).

The firm's ability to finance intended future operations also requires investigation. Thus, trends in working capital and in key financial ratios (profit to sales, the current ratio, stock turnover, debtors to creditors, etc) must be monitored. On the manufacturing side, plant productivity, machine and warehouse capacities, the availability of skilled labour and the efficiency of existing scheduling procedures need assessing. The effectiveness of the company's administrative methods and the calibre of its management should also be analysed. See Chapter 3 for further information on these matters.

CHECKLIST
To ensure that proper consideration is given to all the factors relevant to your choice of strategy, answer the following questions.

1. Which outputs contribute most to aggregate profits and why? Is the product with the highest mark-up the best selling of all the firm's outputs, and if not why not?

Adviceline
Consider increasing the turnover of the highest markup product through (1) relating the bonuses paid to marketing personnel to the volume of sales of this product, and (2) offering lucrative special dealership arrangements to distributors.

---

2. Has the company's choice of markets created credit control or other cash flow problems? Would switching markets remove these problems and how much do you estimate the changeover would cost?
3. Why should any customer buy from you and not from a competing

business? What are the three essential selling points of each of your major products?

4. How do you think your suppliers, junior employees, the bank and other creditors view your firm? Which of their perceptions do you regard as positive and which negative? What caused the supposed negative feelings about the business and how might these be altered?

Adviceline

The simplest way to establish how suppliers and other outsiders regard your company is to ask them. Draft a few simple questions about how they find your goods-inwards and payments systems, how easily they can contact key people within the firm, the images that your letterheads, telephone switchboard, etc, create in their minds, and so on. Put these questions to a small sample of suppliers and customers.

---

5. How many methods of distributing your goods, other than the ones you are using at present, are available to the company? Have the advantages and disadvantages of alternative channels of distribution been fully explored, and if not why not?

6. What proportion of your equipment is genuinely up to date and how much needs replacing? What are the long-run implications of your plant and equipment situation?

7. For how many years can you reasonably expect existing products to sell without having to alter their design or contents?

8. How quickly do you learn about:
   — the effectiveness of each of your advertising campaigns;
   — competitors' price changes and other alterations in competitors' behaviour;
   — the responsiveness of sales to price cuts or promotional activity?

Adviceline

Make one of your junior colleagues personally responsible for monitoring each of the above and for preparing concise and informative summaries of the information gathered.

---

9. How recently did you examine the efficiency of the firm's organisation and accountability systems? If the answer is 'A long time ago', why have you neglected this important duty?

10. Has the company prepared contingency plans for expanding or winding down its business? If not why not?

Adviceline

Managing growth is potentially the most problematic aspect of strategic management. All sorts of difficulties can emerge: warehousing and stock control problems, rapid expansion of credit sales accompanied by cash flow deficiencies, labour shortages, disruption of existing administrative systems, escalating input costs, inadequacies in distribution systems, etc. Conspicuous expansion, moreover, indicates that your business is doing well and operating in highly profitable markets. This signals to other companies that lucrative opportunities exist in your field, hence attracting fresh and unwelcome competition.

Accordingly, you need to prepare detailed forecasts of the costs, revenues and cash flow implications of possible expansions of (say) 10 per cent, 25 per cent, 50 and 100 per cent of your current output. Identify potential bottlenecks, administrative problems, necessary alterations in distribution systems, space limitations, inadequacies in premises, competitors' reactions, etc.

3

What Can Your Business Do?

Introduction

Every business is particularly good at some things and not so good at others. Helping you to identify your firm's special competencies is the major purpose of this chapter. After reading the following material you should be able to:

- recognise the activities you can and cannot complete satisfactorily;
- implement procedures for improving the capabilities of departments, individual employees and the enterprise generally;
- appreciate the sources of the competitive advantage of your firm;
- improve co-ordination within the business;
- assess whether management training is really worthwhile;
- decide whether acquiring other enterprises will increase levels of competence and profitability within the company.

What competence is

There is a crucial difference between the specific operational abilities that a business possesses (marketing, production or quality control, for example) and its level of competence taken as a whole. To illustrate this, consider the depressingly familiar phenomenon of a football or cricket team that comprises 11 enormously talented (and hugely expensive) individual players but which, nevertheless, finds it impossible collectively to win a game! Conversely, teams of essentially mediocre individuals sometimes achieve (through their combined energy, sound organisation, co-ordination and mutual support) spectacular victories. The fact that a business employs highly trained, qualified and motivated people does not *of itself* guarantee success.

Checkpoint

Have you ever managed a project for which you did everything correctly but which, nevertheless, eventually collapsed? Analysing the causes of such failures can be extremely difficult. The best people might have been used, resources may have been more than adequate; enormous care could have been taken when planning the project and monitoring its progress – yet the project still failed.

Poor co-ordination and neglecting to relate individual projects to the business's mission (see Chapter 2) are frequently to blame in these cases. Why this is so is explained later in this chapter (see pages 38–42).

Organisational competence

Examples of organisational competence include:

— the ability to complete projects beyond the capacities of competing businesses;
— acquisition of patents, designs and/or valuable trademarks;
— exceptional proficiency in product research or development;
— technical knowledge;
— the capacity to vary production volume and methods at will;
— abilities to move among different markets quickly and easily.

The *strength* of a firm's ability in each of these areas depends on the following factors:

● whether the special ability relies on a few key personnel continuing to work for the company, or whether it is firmly embedded within the infrastructure and culture of the firm (so that it is passed on from one generation of employees to the next);
● the difficulties that other businesses will experience in obtaining the ability or exercising it to the same level of proficiency;
● whether the ability can be continuously improved to meet contemporary requirements;
● the extent of the gap between your company's level of competence and that of your nearest competitor, and how long it will take that business to match your current abilities.

——————————————— *Checkpoint* ———————————————

List four competencies similar to the previously mentioned examples possessed by your business. How 'strong' are these in terms of the criteria discussed in the last section?

Operational skills and functions

A 'skill' is a capacity to do something proficiently. Normally, several different types of skill are necessary to perform a particular 'function' (manufacturing, accounting, selling or managing personnel, for instance). Consider, for example, the human resources management function of a large organisation. This requires interviewing skills, job evaluation and appraisal skills, manpower planning skills, etc. Each of these in turn requires the input of further skills of a lower order. Thus, for instance, interviewing involves the skills of analysing and interpreting information, listening, communicating, and so on. Specific operational skills may be categorised as follows:

- technical skills involving physical objects or processes (machining, for example);
- information processing skills, ie, those concerned with the discovery and dissemination of data;
- decision-taking skills and problem-solving procedures;
- interpersonal skills required to communicate effectively and lead a team.

----------------- *Checkpoint* -----------------

Considering your firm's mission, rate on a scale of 1 to 5 your company's level of competence for each of the following:

1. Application of modern management methods ☐

2. Fast transmission of important information within the firm ☐

3. Ability to solve problems in a logical and systematic manner ☐

4. Technical ability, eg technical know-how, use of
   up-to-date production methods etc. ☐

Compare your answers with your assessment of the same competencies for your major competitor. What does the analysis tell you about the quality of the firm's forward planning and development systems over the last few years?

Corporate ability development programmes

It is the *totality* of a business's particular skills, acting in unison, which determines its general competence and capacity to outperform the competition. Here are some possible strategies for improving corporate competence.

(a) *Encouragement of learning by doing within the enterprise.* Japanese companies have long enjoyed a significant advantage over Western rivals on account of their provision of security of employment to managerial (and other) personnel, thus creating the need for numerous lateral transfers during an employee's career. (The higher an individual progresses within the same organisation, the fewer opportunities for further promotion exist, so the longer he or she must remain on the same grade.) Accordingly, Japanese managers experience many internal job changes within the same corporation, usually spending (at least) a couple of years in each of several departments: production, marketing, personnel, etc. In consequence they acquire broad perspectives on management and on the overall capacities of their firms. Job rotation, continuous training and slow but steady progression through the managerial hierarchy develop generalist management abilities and 'well-rounded' executives.

(b) *Specialisation and standardisation of products and functions.* Arguably, the best managed companies are those which specialise heavily in their choice of what they will do (the reader may like to consult T J Peters and R H Waterman, *In Search of Excellence*, Harper & Row, London, 1983, in this connection), hence developing great expertise in a particular area. However, all the benefits of diversification (risk-spreading, availability of lucrative opportunities in several fields, etc) are then lost. Another problem with heavy specialisation is its implicit assumption that the more you know about something the better at it you become. This need not be true. Moreover, existing techniques and attitudes are passed on from one generation of employee to the next, including outdated and irrelevant attitudes and working methods. Excessive specialisation can encourage acquiescent and uncritical outlooks, with insufficient analysis, much resistance to change and unquestioning acceptance of the status quo.

(c) *Increasing senior employees' awareness of new environmental opportunities.* Managers need to be sensitive to openings created by (among other things) changes in technology, the emergence of new markets, or the availability of new channels for distributing goods. Hiring employees with experience of other industries and organisations and arranging for internal staff exchanges between divisions and subsidiaries of the same firm can be useful devices for generating appropriate attitudes in this respect. More fundamentally, the *culture of the business* is crucially important in determining how employees respond to change. This is explored in Chapter 8.

(d) *Aiming for high market share rather than short-term profitability.* Capturing the dominant share of a market may not lead to the highest return on capital employed, but it does create stability for the organisation and job security for its workers. Hence, employees are retained for long periods, and it thus becomes worthwhile to train and develop them. Consequently, employees become more able and the company's overall level of competence increases.

(e) *Gap analysis.* This is the means whereby you establish targets based on what seems reasonably attainable in the longer term and then compare them with forecasts derived from the projection of current activities into the future, assuming present circumstances remain unaltered. This enables you to analyse divergences and specify the extra skills the organisation requires in order to bridge the gaps.

Skills and missions

If you know what the organisation exists to do, you can readily define the skills it requires to accomplish its objectives. It is essential, therefore, that the organisation's mission (see Chapter 2) is specified precisely. Then you can initiate schemes for developing these competencies. Equally, however, if your initial suppositions about the company's mission are mistaken, *any* skills improvement programme is bound to fail.

Each company has a unique set of skills and resources that it needs to relate to its market opportunities. If skills and resources are inadequate, actions are necessary to remedy the situation. These may be internal – for example, better co-ordination and/or developing the competence and capacities of existing staff; or external, through the recruitment of extra employees (see Chapter 7) or by acquiring or merging with other firms.

Internal measures

Effective co-ordination of the organisation's activities is the key to improving its overall level of competence, since co-ordination brings together all the individual and functional competencies present within the firm.

--- *Checkpoint* ---

How effective is your business at coping with several serious problems at the same time? Have the solutions to some problems been readily transferred to the solution of others? If not, your company may have a co-ordination problem. Read on to see how this might be overcome.

Co-ordination

Co-ordination means the unification of effort, ie, ensuring that everyone within the enterprise is working towards a common goal.

--- *Checkpoint* ---

Does your company have a formal policy for co-ordinating activity? If not why not?

Adviceline

To be good at co-ordination you have to be good at control, ie, setting operational targets (see Chapter 5), monitoring and evaluating performance and implementing measures to remedy deficiencies. Accordingly, the organisation requires sound information gathering and reporting procedures, an effective appraisal system, and an efficient system for rapid intervention to deal with shortcomings.

The commonest co-ordination technique is the preplanned and systematic delegation of duties to subordinates.

Delegation

In a public company, shareholders delegate to an (elected) board of directors the authority to formulate strategies. Directors then delegate work to heads of department, who in turn delegate particular assignments to individual managers.

Adviceline

Efficient delegation requires a formal system for ensuring that:

- only the right tasks are delegated (it would be ridiculous, for instance, to delegate important decision-taking duties to junior employees while top managers spend their time on low-level activities);
- employees who receive delegated work are trained and competent to complete it properly;
- subordinates are given the resources, information and executive authority necessary to complete delegated tasks;
- the delegation system is carefully dovetailed into a wider staff development programme, so that tasks of increasing difficulty are delegated, thus gradually improving the employee's capacity to undertake higher level work;
- only duties within the normal chain of command are delegated (eg, it would be wrong to expect departmental supervisors to become responsible for dismissing workers);
- senior managers support the decisions of the subordinates to whom work is delegated, even if subordinates' decisions are sometimes wrong (otherwise, junior managers will become extremely reluctant to take important decisions).

Delegation procedures should be formal and recorded. If they are not, staff changes and altered job descriptions can confuse the

---

question of who exactly is responsible for various delegated tasks. A manager who resigns might not inform his or her replacement of the fact that a particular duty has been delegated. Hence, jobs remain unfinished and unpleasant arguments arise among members of staff.

Co-ordination systems

Co-ordination systems may be temporary or permanent. The latter include the following:

1. Appointment of a full-time liaison manager whose main duty is the co-ordination of the work of several departments. The problem here is deciding to whom this person should report. If the co-ordinator outranks each of the heads of participating departments, the status of the department heads will be lowered. If, conversely, the liaison manager is accountable to a head of department, that department may be seen by others as occupying a special and undeservedly privileged position.

Adviceline

Use of a junior manager to co-ordinate activities is rarely satisfactory. Admittedly, this person gains extensive experience of general business management, of dealing with interpersonal conflict, motivating others, work scheduling, etc, and typically will apply great effort and enthusiasm to the work; but junior managers inevitably face situations where they must take decisions against the advice of more senior colleagues, and doing this may threaten a junior manager's career. Doubts, ambiguity and equivocation then follow.

A senior person has the formal authority to ensure that all necessary tasks are actually completed, regardless of the views of heads of department. Unfortunately, however, senior managers rarely possess the time (or possibly the interest) necessary to administer all the important detail attached to major projects. Hence, they might take decisions haphazardly, without completing proper analysis or background research.

This dilemma can develop into an extremely serious problem, for which no clear-cut solution may be advanced. Either a senior person must solemnly undertake to devote proper care and attention to the co-ordination of a project, or the task must be delegated to a junior manager – *accompanied by* a definite promise that his or her decisions will always be implemented.

2. Creation of a permanent task force to co-ordinate activities. Each member of the task force will represent a participating department or interest group. The problem, of course, is that conflicts may arise between a person's departmental loyalty and his or her responsibility to the project as a whole.

Temporary systems

Temporary systems may involve the use of an ad hoc co-ordinator (usually a senior manager) seconded from one of the firm's functional departments for a short time. Such a manager needs to be well known and (ideally) popular among those whose work he or she is to co-ordinate. The short-term nature of the assignment will usually mean that the co-ordinating manager needs to rely more on persuasion and informal contacts than on formal authority to achieve results.

Another possibility is to employ an external consultant on a short-term contract. This solves the difficulties that sometimes arise from conflicts of loyalties facing internal staff, but the detailed knowledge of day-to-day operations possessed by internal employees is lost.

Adviceline

Confronted with a choice between a single-person co-ordinator and a committee, always select the single person. Committees have been described as comprising 'the unfit, appointed by the unwilling to do the unnecessary', and there is much justification in this view. Effective co-ordination requires quick decisions, firm action, and a willingness to assume responsibility. Committees are rarely the best medium for achieving these ends.

Gathering information

The efficiency of a co-ordination system depends critically on the supply of relevant and reliable *information*, which may be obtained through formal or informal means. Formal communication channels involve reports, memoranda, committee meetings, one-to-one discussions, etc. Informal channels include 'the grapevine' (gossip, rumours, unofficial written communications) and what has come to be known as 'management by walking around' (see Peters and Waterman on this – details on page 37).

Management by walking around

How much do you know about what really goes on within your organisation? Objective setting, appraisal, accountability systems, etc, are fine for establishing procedures and monitoring progress; but too often they fail to provide the detailed and accurate information on day-to-day operations and (most important) on staff morale necessary for effective control. Management by walking around (MBWA) is a devastatingly simple solution to the problem of gathering information about actual behaviour within a firm. You look and listen, talk to people, and become personally involved with happenings at your subordinates' places of work. More specifically, MBWA concerns:

- reviewing and appraising sources of information;
- looking for new and better contacts;
- learning how people (senior managers as well as junior employees) *feel* about the organisation and each other;
- finding out how the staff perceive customers, and assessing whether they recognise a personal responsibility for customer care.

The quality of management

A firm is nothing without its workers, but workers must themselves be organised and managed. The primary strength of a business is, therefore, the quality of its management.

―――――――――――――― *Checkpoint* ――――――――――――――

Write a list of at least ten words or phrases which in your view accurately describe the qualities possessed by a good manager. The list might include words such as: resourcefulness, creativity, independence, etc. Review your list when you have read the next section.

Ideally, managers should have a comprehensive knowledge of the company, its trading environment, products, production methods, markets and personnel. They should know all the firm's major administrative procedures and specialist techniques. They need, moreover, to be able to co-ordinate, plan, delegate, establish priorities, lead and control, motivate and communicate, solve problems, identify opportunities, and initiate new work. They also need a working knowledge of important laws on employment, consumer protection, and health and safety.

Desirable personal qualities in a manager are the abilities to assume responsibility, cope with stress, placate angry colleagues, take decisions quickly yet analytically, and willingly accept new ideas.

―――――――――――――― *Checkpoint* ――――――――――――――

Using the above as yardsticks, how many of your senior colleagues are 'good' managers? (It is rare indeed for a manager to satisfy even a majority of the previously mentioned criteria.) Considering the particular shortcomings of your senior colleagues, can you identify a common theme running through their deficiencies and, if so, what is the cause of this?

How can an organisation create within its senior employees a set of effective managerial skills? There is no easy answer to this question. It depends in part on the firm's recruitment and promotion policies (see Chapter 6), its culture (see Chapter 8), its remuneration and other motivation systems, and on how it trains and develops its managerial personnel.

Management training
Is it worthwhile spending money on management training? On the one hand, training can significantly improve the skills of individual managers, equip them for more senior and demanding roles, and improve morale and flexibility throughout the organisation. On the other hand, training is expensive and time-consuming, and there is no guarantee of positive benefits.

Adviceline

Avoid 'gifted amateur' approaches to management training. An example of this, I suggest, is the increasingly popular 'outward bound' type of management/leadership course that involves rock climbing, canoeing, sailing, orienteering, etc. The philosophy behind these courses assumes that there are direct parallels between the personal qualities needed for successful business management and those cultivated by following certain outdoor activities, since both involve leadership, team-building, control, handling stress and uncertainty, organisation, achieving objectives, motivating others, and so on. Participants in such courses, advocates argue, are forced to examine critically their personal strengths and weaknesses, their relationships with others, and the true nature of command.

Unfortunately, outdoor exercises do not help managers to acquire the skills needed to tackle complex management information problems, to interpret complex data, construct analytical decision-taking models, or to deal with information technology related aspects of organisation and control.

Increasingly, the ability to use a computerised system is more important to effective management than many of the previously mentioned interpersonal skills. Arguably, therefore, management training should focus on sophisticated modern techniques rather than canoeing or scrambling up the side of a hill.

Before spending a penny on management training, ask yourself the following questions:

- How exactly will the post-training performance of the person who attends the course help your company to fulfil its mission?
- Will the competencies acquired through attending the course be unique to the individual, or can they be passed on to other people within the organisation?
- How will the course improve the employee's
  - knowledge (what he or she needs to know);
  - personal skill (what he or she needs to be able to do);
  - attitude towards the work of the organisation?
- Will the training ensure that the manager possesses the competencies necessary to meet the firm's *future* needs as well as current requirements?

Adviceline

When considering whether to send an employee on a management training course, always ask yourself the question 'What difference would it make if this training did not take place?' If the answer is 'not much', do not proceed with the training.

Note finally the danger of overtraining your company's managers. Not only may highly trained employees leave the firm if they are unable to use their newly acquired talents, but there is also the possibility that extensive top-quality management training may fine-tune senior executives' critical and reasoning abilities to such an extent that nothing ever actually gets done! Practical, utilitarian and instrumental skills are also needed.

Look to the future

In assessing your company's strengths and weaknesses and hence its skills development requirements, you need to consider not only the options that follow from its *current* activities, but also the feasibility of quite radical changes to products, markets and production methods – to move perhaps from engineering to computers, from textiles to pottery, or from transport to the provision of retailing services.

The question is not so much, 'How can we improve our current operations?', but rather 'What *else* can we do in order to maximise our profits and growth?' Answers may suggest a diversification strategy – new products, new markets and/or the adoption of new technologies;

or a strategy of consolidation of existing market share; seeking to improve profitability through disinvestment in unprofitable activities and/or the acquisition of other firms. You have two basic options:

(a) identify the activities the business performs (or could perform) really well and concentrate on these; or
(b) seek new opportunities in entirely different fields.

The former course assumes that the firm can continue its present operations without hindrance and at peak efficiency, ie, that no discernible threats from competitors, poor industrial relations, interruptions in supplies, or impending technological developments, currently exist. For the second option, realistic opportunities have to be available and the firm must be able to identify them quickly and at low cost. To pursue the latter course, therefore, the organisation may initiate internal research and development programmes, undertake market research, monitor economic trends, and so on.

Checkpoint

- How many new products do you believe your company is capable of introducing over the next five years?
- Might it be possible to alter the shapes, sizes, design or contents of existing output in order to create 'new' products?
- Do you know of any foreign firms which produce and/or market similar goods?

Adviceline

Observing the operations of foreign suppliers of related products is a rich source of ideas about new projects that your own firm might undertake. Much help is available for tracing foreign producers through the Department of Trade and Industry and local Chambers of Commerce.

Diversification and the smaller firm

If you opt for diversification, either your business has to think up completely new products or it must imitate someone else's ideas (though note how attempting to copy other products can itself create the inspiration to develop entirely new goods). It is necessary, of course, to ensure that you do not interfere with an existing patent or breach copyright. Smaller firms sometimes enjoy advantages in these respects because they do not have large amounts of capital locked into particular technologies or administrative or distribution systems and thus are more flexible and better equipped to respond to change.

Planning for change

The business must consider not only the skills it needs for satisfactory performance today, but also the competencies it needs for future operations. This means predicting likely changes in production, legal, marketing and other environments.

Adviceline

There are two ways of planning for environmental change. The first is to predict the external changes that might occur and then detail:

(a) how the organisation would be affected by them; and
(b) how it should respond.

Alternatively, the planner may begin with a list of the firm's existing activities, followed by details of all the environmental factors that could affect these.

Choose the latter course. It is concrete, and named individuals can be made responsible for listing the factors relevant to each activity (production, accounts, distribution, etc). The important thing is to make sure that no important variable is overlooked.

Checkpoint

How quickly and easily could your firm prepare a comprehensive list of the activities and resources needed to adapt to a significant change in one of its environments (entry of a new competitor to an important market, for example)?

All the necessary financial, personnel, technical and other resources would have to be outlined and compared with those currently available. If the business would experience difficulty in collecting and analysing this information, you need to re-examine the adequacy of its management information gathering system.

Acquiring other firms

Buying other businesses is the obvious and frequently the most cost-effective way of enhancing a company's strengths and overcoming its weaknesses. An acquisition may simultaneously achieve several strategic objectives:

(a) It can expand the scope of the business.
(b) The acquired firm may already operate in a lucrative new market, hence saving your company the costs and inconveniences of entering that field independently.

(c) The net worth of the firm is increased.
(d) Diversification across products and markets may be achieved at low cost.
(e) Risks are spread over several activities.

Checkpoint

Write a list of all the types of work your business is competent to undertake (1) now, (2) following a 10 per cent increase in resources.

Other sound reasons for acquiring businesses abound. They include:

- the desire to obtain particular types of productive capacity and/or cash reserves (especially during periods of high interest rates, when the purchase of a cash rich subsidiary paid for by shares in the parent firm can be the cheapest means of improving the parent's liquidity position);
- the fact that it is cheaper and faster to buy than to build;
- the need to develop a 'critical mass' capable of influencing a particular market significantly (selling a small quantity to each of many markets deprives the company of 'critical mass');
- the possibilities of combining distribution channels, using one sales force to sell the output of both companies, labour force savings, joint use of premises and equipment, etc.

Checkpoint

Does your company have experience of selling in diverse markets? Has it ever adapted products to meet the needs of different customer types? Deficiencies in these respects are among the commonest reasons for acquiring other businesses.

Acquisition strategy

First you should specify the objectives of an intended acquisition; for example, to obtain additional resources, enter a new market, guarantee access to sources of supply, or whatever. Then you need to determine the criteria to be used in selecting the target firm. These might include the requirements that:

- the proposed acquisition already possesses well-known brand images within its markets;
- only firms operating in buoyant and rapidly expanding market segments are to be considered;
- the acquisition must have assets that will complement the operations of the parent firm;
- senior employees in the target business must possess certain competencies, experience, qualifications and skills.

Acquisition of strategy checklist
The purpose of an acquisition should be to improve the competitive position (see Chapter 2) of the acquiring company. For instance, it may create possibilities for the expert use of resources (eg, when one firm possesses large amounts of land and buildings and the other is highly skilled in property management), or assist diversification, or help in spreading risk. Ask the following questions in respect of each candidate for acquisition.

- How exactly will the acquired firm help the organisation to fulfil its mission?
- Which of your company's internal weaknesses (research, distribution, lack of warehousing space, etc) will the acquisition overcome?
- Are the cultures (see Chapter 8) and working methods of the two businesses compatible?
- Does the target firm genuinely possess experience of products and markets that you could not obtain at low cost without the acquisition?
- Will the acquisition lead to reductions in operating cost via integration of processes, bulk buying, etc?
- Will the acquisition improve your control over distribution channels or supplies?
- Are there any tax considerations attached to the exercise; for example, the carryover of the target company's past trading losses to your own books?
- Is your current management team capable of running two businesses at the same time? Can it handle the new technologies and/or management methods the acquisition will bring? What are the implications of the larger scale of operations for your company's appraisal and management information systems?

Adviceline
In most circumstances you should handle the purchase of another business inconspicuously, avoiding publicity where you can. The publicity surrounding an acquisition may alert trade competitors to your diversification/expansion plans and cause them to interfere with the project (eg, by setting up their own subsidiary to compete in the markets of the acquired firm).

CHECKLIST
Assess the strengths of your business as *either* 'excellent' or 'less than excellent' in each of the following categories:

Selling and distribution

Buying
Collecting information and conducting research
Internal communications
Stockkeeping
Quality control
Packaging and dispatch
Ability to deliver on time
After-sales service
Public relations and the ability to project a favourable image
Advertising and promotions
Monitoring market trends
Dealer support
Planning future activities
Use of premises (allocation of space, maintenance, etc)
Control over manufacturing costs
Control over distribution costs
Labour relations
Credit control
Relations with suppliers of finance (the bank, etc)
Managerial knowledge of day-to-day operations
Ability to manage unusual ad hoc projects
Efficient use of equipment
Ability to take important decisions quickly
Level of motivation of employees.

Now count up the number of items in each category. What does the result tell you about your competitive position? How do you think your major competitors would score on this analysis?

Write out three reasons to explain each of your 'less than excellent' assessments. What can be done to improve the situation for these items?

4

Organising for Bigger Profits

Introduction

A business organisation is put together from constituent elements. You must create departments, decide who is to be accountable to whom, establish divisions, determine whether individual and departmental responsibilities are to overlap, and select appropriate methods for controlling the activities of the various sections of the firm. After reading this chapter you should be able to:

- identify the sources of organisational problems within your business;
- understand the options available for designing organisations;
- devise a sensible organisation structure for your firm;
- decide whether to centralise or decentralise your business's operations.

--------------------------------- *Checkpoint* ---------------------------------

List the ten major activities (eg, manufacturing a certain product, preparing final accounts, selling to retail outlets, etc) that your company undertakes, in order of how you see their importance. Does the way that your business is organised ensure that top priority is given to the highest ranking activities? For example, is more information generated on these activities than on others? Are resources and the attention of key personnel directed towards these crucial tasks?

Identifying organisational problems

Many factors create the need to restructure an organisation: rapid expansion, alterations in production or other technologies, a new corporate mission, changes in company law, and so on. Signs of organisational inadequacy include:

- management not being able to appraise the efficiencies of certain functions (accounting, marketing, etc) or activities (eg, launching a

product, changing a production technique) because of the complexity of organisational interrelationships within the firm;
- staff not knowing the organisation's true objectives;
- absence of procedures for interdepartmental consultation and/or joint departmental decision-taking;
- a single favoured department dominating others, even to the extent that other departments feel they require its permission prior to initiating certain actions;
- conflicts between individual and organisational goals, and the pursuit by individuals of personal rather than company objectives;
- slow and ineffective decision-taking within the business;
- excessive numbers of meetings necessitated by people not being sure what they are expected to do;
- poor co-ordination of projects;
- non-implementation of strategic plans.

———————————————— *Checkpoint* ————————————————

Ask a sample of your firm's employees the following questions:

(a) Do they ever feel that conflicting demands are imposed on them by different managers?
(b) Are they completely clear about the scope and responsibilities of their jobs?
(c) Do they consider that they receive all the information necessary for completing their assignments?
(d) Do they regard the division of labour within the organisation as:
— rigid or flexible;
— conducive to the company achieving its goals?

Management must choose (1) how to segment the business into appropriate working units and (2) how to integrate and co-ordinate the configurations that emerge. The former involves the design of the organisation, the latter is about how centrally the organisation is to be controlled.

Adviceline

Remember that organisational designs result from human effort and ingenuity and not from chance. Someone consciously determines the form of a business's organisation. Were this not the case the firm could not exist, since it would never have been created in the first instance!

'Structure', a trade union leader once declared, 'should be a function of purpose'. This is very true; the organisational details of any enterprise – public or private, business or trade union, co-operative, government agency or whatever – should relate

---

> immediately and directly to the attainment of strategic objectives. Thus, confronted with a choice among alternative types of organisation structure, you should decide which to adopt by simply asking yourself the question, 'Which of these arrangements is best for helping the company to fulfil its mission?'

How organisations develop

As firms age and develop they tend to progress through similar organisational crises and in consequence to adopt similar organisational arrangements. Usually, a business is founded by one or two owners who personally control all its work and who dominate its organisation. Then the enterprise begins to expand and for the first time paid employees are needed. Each recruit is put under the immediate authority of one of the owners, leading to extremely wide 'spans of control' within the business.

Spans of control

A manager's span of control is the number of direct subordinates he or she possesses. Narrow spans involve just two or three immediate subordinates; wide spans have perhaps 15 or 20. The problem with a wide span is that many subordinates will be seeking the manager's attention simultaneously, each requesting instructions and proffering advice. Managers become overwhelmed with work in these circumstances and unable to control their departments effectively.

Accordingly, each manager's span of control needs to be narrowed so that he or she has to deal only with a small number of subordinates, but can do so properly.

Adviceline

Choosing the best span of control is not as simple as it first appears. Wide spans have advantages as well as drawbacks.

- They force managers to delegate (hence providing subordinates with experience of higher-level work).
- Employees' job satisfaction may increase.
- There are fewer levels of authority within the firm.

The following rules of thumb may be useful for selecting the appropriate number of subordinates for each manager.

(a) Complex work usually requires a narrow span of control because of the time and effort needed to consider the ideas and information submitted by subordinates.

(b) Efficient internal communications enable the application of wider spans (managers and subordinates can contact each other quickly and easily to sort out difficulties).
(c) Well-educated, enthusiastic and competent subordinates require less control. Hence, more of them may be effectively supervised at any one moment.

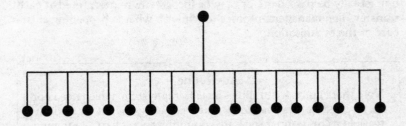

(a) Wide span of control

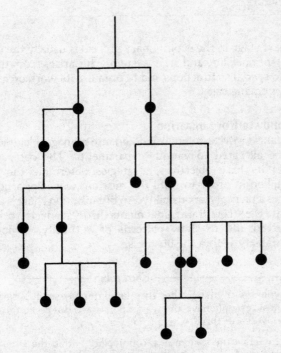

(b) Narrow span of control

Figure 4.1

Typically, businesses do narrow their spans of control as operations expand. Consequently, they move from the sort of situation depicted in Figure 4.1(a) to that shown in Figure 4.1(b) on page 55. Unfortunately, narrow spans create many levels of authority within the system, resulting in long (and potentially fragile) chains of communication and control. Important information has to pass through the hands of many people during its transmission through the structure. Information may not actually be passed on, or may be incorrectly reinterpreted at each transfer. Top management loses touch with what is happening at the base of the organisation.

Adviceline

Note that Figure 4.1(b) shows an *authority* system, which need not correspond to the *business's communication system*. It is entirely feasible to draw up a separate communication chart – outlining who may communicate directly with whom. This chart will involve the same people but will have a completely different structure.

The next stage in the evolutionary process is usually the emergence of a conventional 'line and staff' system. This arises from the company's need to specialise functions and to organise its work on a more formal and systematic basis.

Line and staff organisation

To organise work is to break it down into manageable units which may then be allocated to various departments. The company's mission dictates its base objectives; strategies determine the work to be undertaken in order to fulfil the mission; work apportionment then becomes a tactical responsibility. An organisation chart is an attempt to illustrate the structural arrangements through which work allocation is to proceed and to show patterns of authority, responsibility and accountability within the business.

Checkpoint

If yours is anything other than an extremely small business it will almost certainly have an organisation chart. But do you really know the *purposes* of this document. They are:

- to define the system of accountability within the enterprise and hence who may delegate work to whom;
- to inform each individual of the person whose instructions he or she should obey.

The latter is particularly important, because demarcations between departmental and personnel responsibilities can become extremely confused, resulting in subordinates receiving conflicting instructions from several different superiors. Accordingly, the principle of 'unity of command' is usually applied to these systems. This is the axiom that each person should have only one boss, thus avoiding the (severe) difficulties created by instructions being issued to the same person from different sources.

Do you have unity of command within your organisation? Note how in theory an employee may be responsible to a single superior, but that in practice he or she may take more notice of someone else. If this occurs in your business you should investigate why it is happening.

Line managers take decisions and issue instructions. Staff managers (personnel managers or company lawyers are good examples) give advice but do not possess executive authority to implement major decisions. Internal specialisation increases, but the organisation becomes rigid and (most important) incapable of changing its working methods. Decisions taken by the firm's various functional departments begin to conflict and the existing line and staff system becomes increasingly irrelevant to what actually happens.

The fact that the firm has taken the trouble to draft an organisation chart does not necessarily help in these circumstances, since organisation charts illustrate only a *desired* organisation structure at a specific moment and do not reveal interdepartmental rivalries, office politics, personal favouritism, or differences in senior management's perceptions of the calibres of various employees. Business environments change continuously, and organisations must respond quickly to new situations.

Several factors may contribute to the demise of a conventional line and staff system, including:

- concentration of power in the hands of just a few line managers and hence the reliance of the entire system on a handful of key people;
- irreconcilable conflicts between line managers and their staff advisers;
- emergence of informal and unofficial systems of authority and communication;
- too heavy a concentration of decision-making at the top of the organisation (ie, middle managers perhaps finding it too easy to refer problems upwards for final resolution);
- line managers becoming overwhelmed with advice;
- staff specialists seeking to circumvent and undermine line managers' authority.

Adviceline

If you operate a conventional line and staff system, keep your staff managers firmly under control. Do *not* allow them partial authority to implement decisions, because enormous co-ordination and control problems could then ensue. Staff specialists should be too busy keeping abreast of their professional subjects to worry about executive management! Relationships become highly complicated and responsibilities unclear; staff/line manager communications collapse, and there is much duplicated effort. Aim for a simple and unambiguous chain of command with clearly delineated responsibilities.

At this stage in its development the business will (or should) ask itself a number of searching questions about the adequacy of its current organisational arrangements. Decentralisation will be considered, and the firm will actively search for new and (possibly) more flexible organisational forms.

Decentralisation

There is perhaps a natural tendency for organisations to decentralise as they expand, since this allows 'local' control over operations while leaving top management free to devote all its attention to long-term strategic plans.

Decentralisation may occur through the creation of subsidiary companies or through the divisionalisation of a single firm. In a tightly controlled decentralised organisation, an inner administrative body takes all significant decisions and issues *binding* directives to divisions (or subsidiaries). Divisional managers follow predetermined rules and procedures, exercising little discretion over how they complete their work. Note that the larger the organisation, the harder it becomes for top management to take all important decisions affecting divisions, so that some delegation of divisional authority has to occur.

Loose decentralisation

The aims of loose decentralisation are improved efficiency, less red tape, better divisional decision-taking and faster response to environmental change. In a loosely controlled system, decisions are taken by divisional/departmental managers who possess intimate knowledge of 'local' conditions, within budgetary constraints imposed by central management. Typically, divisional heads are given targets by the centre in the context of an overall corporate plan, but are then left to achieve objectives in their own ways.

The advantages of divisionalisation include (1) the motivation of divisional managers who use their own initiative in solving problems, (2) its value in training local managers for more senior central posts, and (3) the relative ease with which divisional activities can be integrated by the central control. The disadvantages are (1) the duplication of effort involved, (2) losses of economies of scale and specialisation, and (3) the possibility of divisions regarding themselves as independent bodies with objectives different from those of the parent firm. Rivalries between divisions may emerge, with divisions vying for attention and additional resources.

Adviceline

In deciding the extent of the decentralisation within your company (all organisations are necessarily decentralised to some degree), ask yourself the following questions:

- Is top management genuinely capable of adopting a global view of all the company's resources and operations (aggregate cash flows, deployment of labour between sections, etc)? If so, *more* rather than less decentralisation is appropriate because individual units may then be left to manage themselves in the context of an effective overall strategic plan drawn up and effectively co-ordinated by the central control.
- Does the information generated by decentralised units facilitate accurate planning of their activities? Indicators of this are: (1) whether section budgets are regularly over- or underspent, and (2) whether predicted returns from investments within units are actually realised.

  The less reliable the information that emerges from decentralised units the greater the need for centralisation, since managers at the centre need to be able to intervene quickly in order to redeploy resources around the organisation; for example, by abandoning low-return investments initiated by decentralised units.
- Are departmental and other sectional managers truly competent to take important decisions and govern their own affairs? If they are not, you may be better off training and developing them than centralising the organisation. Implementation of a centralisation policy greatly increases the workloads of head office managers.
- Do managers at head office possess skills and special abilities that sectional managers cannot possibly obtain?

Other points to bear in mind are that (1) the greater the degree of centralisation the more staff have to be employed at the centre, and (2) the greater the competence of central managers the more dependent on the centre will 'local' managers become (they will refer *all* difficult problems to the central control).

An important danger with decentralisation is the possibility that certain managers in decentralised units, who dislike how these units are run, may attempt to establish direct links with head office in order to undermine the authority of their superiors in the decentralisation units in which they are employed. Usually, decentralisation is most appropriate for firms producing a limited range of products, with integrated systems and much standardisation of working methods.

Appraising divisions

An important task when creating divisions is to ensure that their performances can be easily measured and appraised, since sometimes one or more divisions subsidise others without anyone being aware of the fact. Problems attached to devising an appraisal scheme for divisions include:

- deciding whether each division is to be regarded as a cost centre in its own right (hence 'buying in' materials and services from other divisions);
- choice of criteria for measuring profitability (absolute money values, rates of return on capital employed, etc);
- assessing the effects of company policies on the profits made by a particular division (eg, the effects of artificially low input prices from other divisions);
- overhead allocations relating to shared common services (administrative premises, for instance) and relating these to estimates for divisional rates of return on capital employed;
- deciding whether divisions should manage their own idle cash balances or turn them over to a central treasury for investment outside the division (externally or elsewhere in the company);
- how to establish an efficient system for setting divisional targets and budgets, ie how to inaugurate a divisional management by objectives scheme.

Strategic business units

This is a term coined by American strategists to denote groupings of a business's activities which are then treated as self-contained entities for the purposes of strategic planning and control. A strategic business unit (SBU) could be a division of a company, a department, a collection of departments, a subsidiary, or a function undertaken within a firm (eg, all the firm's marketing activities might be regarded as an independent SBU). Often, SBUs cut across existing divisional, functional and departmental boundaries.

Having defined SBUs, management then gives each unit a budget and the authority to administer its own resources. The idea was invented by the US General Electric company which, dissatisfied with its existing divisional structure, rearranged all the enterprise's activities into SBUs, some of which bore little relation to traditional departments, divisions or profit centres. Thus, for example, a number of food preparation appliances previously manufactured and sold through several independent divisions were merged into a single 'housewares' SBU.

Similarly, a firm might produce television sets in one division, radios in the next, and car stereo systems in another. Yet for strategy and planning purposes all three activities could be conveniently lumped together into a single SBU.

―――――――――― *Checkpoint* ――――――――――

Can you identify obvious SBUs within your business that do not correspond to existing divisions or departments? If you can, how do you justify not having created divisions/departments corresponding to these SBUs in the first place?

To make sense, an SBU should:

- comprise compatible elements, each possessing a direct and identifiable link with the unit as a whole;
- be easily appraised (which requires that its performance needs to be compared with something similar either within or outside the organisation);
- contribute significantly towards the attainment of the company's mission.

The obvious problems, of course, are how to co-ordinate many disparate activities and how to assess the financial and other contributions of each activity to the SBU.

Flexible versus formal structures

An organisation that operates within fast changing environments may have to alter its organisational structure at short notice and for all aspects of its work. Consider, for instance, a computer manufacturing company which finds, unexpectedly, that a competitor has introduced a cheaper and superior model. This business must completely reorganise its design, production, marketing and administration systems – almost at once. Thus, it should adopt a flexible organisation structure, with total labour mobility, overlapping responsibilities (so that people can be quickly and easily replaced), and fragile and transitory departmental arrangements that can be altered at will. Employees must be capable of undertaking different types of work and be culturally attuned to accepting change.

Conversely, organisations which are in relatively stable environments, or which employ poorly educated and/or apathetic staff, or which involve routine assembly line or similarly mundane activities that *cannot* be made more interesting, may opt for rigid formal and bureaucratic organisational forms. Rules will exist covering every aspect of the company's work. There are clear divisions of work and responsibility, and extremely close supervision. All procedures are standardised and written out in instruction manuals; workers exercise minimal discretion over how they undertake their tasks. Relationships are extremely formal; all the workers know their place and exactly what they are expected to do.

Such measures relieve employees of the burden of having to think for themselves, and there is a high probability that work will be completed on time. But individual initiative is stifled and this type of organisation is not remotely capable of accommodating change – people 'pass the buck' whenever they are confronted by new ideas. Work is a ritual; employees adhere to current practices and will only do as they are told, never suggesting new ideas. Staff lose sight of the organisation's strategic goals. They behave as they have in the past and apply outdated solutions to problems: the ability to stick to the detailed minutiae of existing working methods becomes an end in itself.

Adviceline

Adopt the following procedure for dealing with bureaucracy and red tape in a small firm:

(a) Prepare a comprehensive inventory of all the forms and other standard documents (customer advice notes, for instance) used by the organisation. Then ask the following questions in relation to each document:
— why is it necessary;
— who uses the data it contains;
— what objectives does it seek to achieve;
— what would happen if it ceased to exist?
Eliminate all forms and documents that no longer serve a useful purpose. Combine as many as possible of those which remain.

(b) Have departmental managers list and describe the purposes of each of their departments' substantive activities. Sometimes, the need for a departmental operation originated in another department that no longer exists; yet the procedure continues simply because employees are ignorant of its initial aim.

(c) Examine the levels of skill, training and experience needed to undertake various departmental operations. Can the work be done by less skilled and experienced (and thus cheaper) people?

(d) From the lists of activities compiled in step (b), identify duplicated effort, possible cost savings and the overall sequence of activities within the firm. Eliminate redundant procedures and integrate as many others as you can.

Do this thoroughly and you will greatly reduce the transit time needed for work to move through the organisation.

Designing an organisation

Begin by considering the basic *functions* that your organisation structure will have to serve. These are:

- to have the right people taking the right decisions at the right time;
- to establish who is accountable for what and who reports to whom;
- to facilitate the easy flow of information through the organisation;
- to provide a working environment that encourages efficiency and the acceptance of change;
- to integrate and co-ordinate activities.

Adviceline

The issue of whether the existence of 'organisational slack' within businesses is good or bad is difficult to resolve. Efficiency requires that everyone works hard and that the firm has no idle resources. Arguably, however, rigid routines and constant shortages of time caused by 100 per cent capacity use inhibit initiative and the emergence of creative new ideas. Managers do not have time to reflect on fundamental questions in these circumstances.

I believe that a tightly run organisation is preferable to one that is not. The energy and excitement generated by constant activity provide a progressive atmosphere conducive to enterprise and the generation of new ideas. Managers do not necessarily spend their slack periods thinking bold and imaginative thoughts about how to improve the firm. They are just as likely to extend their meal breaks, spend extra time in unproductive meetings, chat to colleagues, and so on.

The chosen structure must balance order and innovation. On the one hand, it must avoid the duplication of effort, standardise procedures, monitor the quality of work, etc. On the other hand, it should encourage initiative among the staff and generate job satisfaction in employees through presenting them with an interesting variety of disparate tasks. There is no single ideal structure that is universally applicable to all businesses. What works in one firm may not be suitable elsewhere because of differences in mission, strategies, and the calibre of personnel.

Now look for natural and self-evident sectional divisions of work. In the ideal situation:

- each unit will act as a self-contained cost/profit centre;
- the performance of units can be easily appraised;
- information about units is readily available (meaning they can be controlled without difficulty);
- units are 'organic' in that each contains homogeneous elements and/or elements with a common purpose (eg, putting all marketing activities together into a single department);
- work passes from one unit to the next in a logical sequence;
- units' resource needs are clearly visible so that resources may be deployed where they are most urgently required.

Adviceline

Sometimes unit managers report that a unit's operations are satisfactory whereas, in fact, its non-managerial employees are desperately short of equipment, materials and time. Unit managers believe that presenting a unit's activities attractively enhances their personal prestige with their own superiors. Yet unit efficiency is bound to decline in the long run.

You need, therefore, a system for direct communication with junior employees in each unit; for example, by involving managers not attached to the unit in question in the appraisal of the performances of its low-ranking staff.

Creating departments

Several options are available for choosing departmental boundaries. The most common are as follows.

Functional structure

This simply means dividing the firm into departments that correspond to common business functions such as manufacturing, finance, marketing, personnel management, and so on. Employees in each department are (or quickly become) skilled specialists in the function it performs. Advantages of the method are that staff are able to tackle complex problems in specific areas, that additional staff may be easily recruited from outside (for example, an accountant can be hired to work in the accounts department and will immediately contribute to departmental tasks), and that functional structure is easy to understand.

Conversely, long periods spent working in a functional department can lead to narrow and introspective attitudes and a failure to recognise the problems and possibilities of the organisation as a whole. Also, much time and effort is needed to co-ordinate the activities of functional departments. Interdepartmental communications may be complicated and slow.

Product structure
This form of departmentation means creating departments each of which deals with a single product or service. Staff control all activities associated with the product, including the purchase of raw materials, administration, processing, and its sale and distribution. Senior departmental managers acquire a wider range of general managerial skills than in functional departments. Co-ordination between the management functions associated with the product is usually quite easy to achieve.

Regional and customer class departments
Another possibility is to create departments covering geographical areas or customer type. Regional sales departments are an example. Local factors can then figure in decision-making, and it may be cheaper to locate offices near to customers. Otherwise, departmentation could relate to customer size (having special facilities for large buyers), retail or wholesale distribution channels, export or home markets, etc. Problems of co-ordination may ensue, and there will be some loss of central control.

Need to keep the organisation up to date
It is not unusual to find companies which continue to operate long-established organisation structures for many years after their missions, strategies and policies have radically changed. Firms should consciously *plan* changes in their organisational systems to keep pace with contemporary operational requirements.

———————————— *Checkpoint* ————————————

How recently has your company reviewed the adequacy of its organisation structure? Such an appraisal should have covered:

- the speed with which information flows through the system;
- the relevance and clarity of current organisation charts and manuals;
- whether work is being delegated in appropriate ways (see Chapter 2);
- relationships between authority and responsibility (are the people held responsible for certain jobs given the authority needed to complete them satisfactorily?);
- the balance between line and staff managers (see page 54) and whether the latter help or hinder the former's work;
- whether there is unnecessary duplication of activities and/or excessive amounts of red tape.

Always remember that the structure of the enterprise is nothing more than a *device* for assisting employees to improve their performance and hence enable the company to fulfil its mission.

Further approaches to organisation

All the previously mentioned organisational systems are well established and have been tried and tested in innumerable industries over many decades. However, new products, new technologies, new markets and increasing competition (especially from overseas) have caused businesses to question the value of orthodox organisational arrangements and to look for more radical solutions to the organisational problems that new technologies raise. Below are listed some further and more recent approaches to organisational design.

Matrix structures (project teams)

Here the firm establishes teams to handle particular functions or assignments. Individuals are seconded from their 'home' departments and thus have a number of bosses: their head of department and the team leaders of the groups to which they are temporarily attached.

Note how matrix organisation deliberately violates the principle of unity of command (see page 55).

Adviceline

Team leaders are responsible for projects, though heads of department retain executive authority over their staff. In consequence, team members may receive conflicting instructions from heads of department and project team leaders. It is important to establish at the outset (1) who, ultimately, each individual should obey, and (2) whether subordinates are to regard themselves first and foremost as members of a department or as members of a

---

particular project team. Usually, departments take precedence since projects last only for limited periods, and individuals will normally be assigned to a number of projects at the same time.

Problems with matrix structure include:

- duplication of activities;
- the need for extensive co-ordination of units (much committee work is involved in an organisation structured on these lines);
- disputes regarding who should do what and who is in charge of whom;
- possible conflicts between the decisions of individual line managers and the collective decisions of project teams (which normally are given their own budgets and authority to implement decisions).

Teams are multidisciplinary, cutting across traditional occupational divisions, departments and distinctions between line and staff. Moreover, matrix structure creates numerous opportunities for employee participation in decision-taking and the rapid development of general managerial skills. The system is extremely flexible (teams can be set up and disbanded at will). Matrix structures are especially useful for:

(a) managing complex projects where immediate access to several highly specialised professional skills is required;
(b) managing strategic business units (see page 58). Often, SBUs do not correspond to existing divisions or departments so that it becomes necessary to establish a team representing each aspect of the work of the unit to oversee its duties.

Honeycomb and motherhood structures

A honeycomb structure comprises a conglomeration of 'cells', each corresponding to a particular functional area. The business recruits employees who are already trained and competent in relevant specialisations, adding or deleting cells as circumstances change. If, for example, a company acquires its own fleet of vehicles it may add a transport management cell to its organisation structure, hiring an experienced and qualified transport manager and associated staff from outside the firm.

The advantage of a honeycomb system is the speed and convenience with which a business can expand or contract its operations (through creating or disbanding cells). Disadvantages are that staff engaged in such a manner will feel little commitment to the enterprise (qualified specialists can easily move to other firms) and labour turnover may be high.

Motherhood systems, conversely, are structured around generalist managers – recruited young and without experience but then trained and developed within the company. Staff become committed to the business, undertake a wide range of duties, experience several types of work and are steeped in the organisation's culture and working practices. There is a coherent management succession scheme and guaranteed continuity of operations within the firm, but employees may lack the detailed knowledge of specialised functions that outside experts possess. Also, because of the long periods necessary to train new entrants, motherhood firms cannot expand or contract their field of activities as readily as honeycomb companies.

Operative cell structure

This is a Japanese idea applicable to manufacturing businesses. In Britain it is usually associated with just-in-time stock control (ie scheduling workflows so precisely that only minimal stocks of work in progress need be held – work from the previous stage in the production process arrives 'just in time'). Workers in each cell are responsible for quality and production control; organise their own work (under supervision); and are put in charge of the repair and maintenance of equipment and the timing of movements of work from one cell to the next.

Operatives' jobs thus become more interesting. Workers function as a team and hence are expected to cover for each other's absences, lateness and so on. Responsibility for errors is shared by the entire group. Errors may lead to lost bonuses for everyone involved.

Adviceline

The success of this type of organisation depends critically on cell members' ability to work as a team, ie to co-operate and *voluntarily* co-ordinate their activities in order to achieve group objectives. There is a need (1) for participants to develop a common bond, (2) for extensive interaction between group members, and (3) for participants to offer mutual support and share common perceptions of events. Achieving these is easier said than done. In particular, a fair distribution of work and responsibility within the group, especially for unpleasant or exceptionally demanding duties, is required. Good supervision is essential, with well-designed work programmes and realistic completion dates for the unit's projects.

Accordingly much time, effort and money needs to be spent on supervisory training. If you simply recruit or promote people into supervisory positions without giving them substantial and high-level supervisory training, you invite the system to collapse.

Networking

Networking is straightforward in principle, though in practice many serious organisational problems are involved. With networking, employees and/or sub-contractors work from home and communicate with head office via a home-based computer, telephone calls, and through face-to-face meetings at prearranged times. Networking is increasingly popular among professional workers who possess a specific technical competence, the exercise of which does not require their physical presence in any particular place. Examples are design, computer programming, technical writing, and similar skills. Indeed anything that can be undertaken from a self-contained home office is amenable to networking. The advantages include:

- the time saved in not having to commute to work (in London this can amount to three or four hours per day);
- a more relaxed working environment leading to greater creativity, more output and a higher level of enthusiasm for work;
- freedom from arbitrary routines, flexible starting and finishing times, absence of set meal breaks, etc (work may be completed when the individual most feels like it);
- not having to endure the numerous unwanted interruptions inevitably attached to working in the head office of a large organisation;
- being able to fit work between transporting children to and from school;
- savings on premises costs for the employing organisation.

A network can be based on either of two quite different employment models. The options are:

(a) to bind the networker to a single firm through paying that person a regular wage, deducting PAYE and Class 1 National Insurance, providing superannuation and perhaps also a company car and other fringe benefits;
(b) treating networkers as self-employed sub-contract labour entirely responsible for their own tax and National Insurance, and paying them an *ad hoc* lump sum fee for each assignment.

In the former case the employer needs systems for (1) periodically appraising networkers' performances, (2) finding new ways of improving efficiency, and (3) generally controlling their efforts. This will involve setting targets, work inspections, home visits by senior managers, etc. Individuals are treated *as if* they were full-time and permanent employees who, circumstantially, do not work at head office.

In the latter (self-employed) situation the firm risks losing the individual to other employers (a networker engaged in this manner has no legal commitment to any particular organisation other than to complete the assignment on hand) and it cannot directly control working methods (if it did the Inland Revenue would not allow the networker to have self-employed status). Assignments are *ad hoc* and the networker has no security of tenure. Particular difficulties arise here if the firm has invested large sums in the networker's training, or if valuable company equipment is used in the networker's home office, or if highly confidential information is involved. The problems of networking include the following:

- Ambiguity of status *vis-à-vis* the employing firm. Networkers are typically employees on long-term and continuing (albeit *ad hoc*) assignments. Yet their work rarely carries the prestige normally attached to a permanent head office post.
- Inability to rise through the ranks of the organisation to a senior line management position. Networkers are specialists and, because of their isolation on the outer fringes of the firm, cannot acquire the general management experience needed for a top job.
- Lack of direct control over networkers. How can head office know the extent of the work actually required to complete a particular job or whether certain work may be deskilled and done elsewhere at lower cost?
- Co-ordination difficulties, especially where projects critically depend on each of several isolated networkers meeting tight deadlines.
- Feelings of insularity, loneliness, and the inability to communicate as frequently as the job requires. Networkers who are constantly on the telephone and/or travelling to see colleagues might just as well work at head office.
- Need to employ head office managers specifically to liaise with networkers, to supply their input requirements, deal with their problems, arrange their meetings, etc.
- Ambiguities regarding the ownership of copyright of ideas, designs, programs, etc, created by networkers at home, especially if the workers are self-employed.

Adviceline

Networking is sure to become increasingly important over the next ten to twenty years. Employees attain far greater control over the pattern of their working lives and the system is much cheaper for employers than hiring head office based full-time permanent staff. Unfortunately, however, UK employment law concerning the legal status of part-time and contract workers, UK superannuation schemes and other company benefit packages,

UK law on intellectual property, and certain other UK laws and customary employment practices are not remotely capable of accommodating the problems and working relationships that networking systems create.

Networking causes the company introducing it to step into a legal minefield, and specialist legal advice on the nature, obligations and implications of explicit or implied contracts of employment with networkers is required.

Who precisely is to be responsible for what? Who is accountable to whom? Who owns the intellectual property emerging from network projects? Is the firm's equipment to be used only for that firm's work? These are just some of the (many) issues that need to be addressed.

CHECKLIST

1. How easily can your senior colleagues conceal their mistakes? If the answer is 'very easily', how might the firm's accountability system be restructured to make obvious the causes and consequences of errors?

Adviceline

Systems which require employees to work in pairs and regularly to exchange their partners are better for identifying the people responsible for numerous mistakes than systems that enable individuals to camouflage their activities behind complex job specifications and intricate organisation structures. A person may succeed in persuading one or two colleagues to collude in covering up his or her persistent incompetence; but the word will quickly spread and the incapable individual will not be able to rely on the indefinite co-operation of several different colleagues.

2. Has the company ever considered questioning its employees to ascertain whether they regard existing divisions of authority and responsibility within the organisation as fair? This can be an extremely useful and revealing exercise.
3. Is it common within your business for managers to be employed as assistants to other managers, without having any clearly discernible responsibilities of their own? If it is, would the firm's capacity to achieve its mission be adversely affected if any or all of these assistants were dismissed, and if so how?
4. How quickly and easily could a junior employee contact a senior manager following an emergency? What does your answer tell you

about the efficiency of your firm's communication system?

5. Does your organisation apply the principle of 'one person one boss'? Does everyone in the business know who his or her real boss actually is? If not why not?

6. Does the firm's organisation structure clearly identify those responsible for (1) formulating strategy, (2) implementing strategy, and (3) controlling day-to-day operations?

7. Does the structure ensure that all the firm's major products receive equal attention from top management? If not, what additional information needs to be transmitted to the apex of the organisation in order to guarantee that senior managers are fully aware of each product's resource needs, and through which channels should this information travel?

8. Do the firm's production and marketing departments communicate regularly? Does each of these departments understand the other's problems?

Adviceline

Staff exchanges between these (and other) departments can be extremely useful for developing empathy in managers for the difficulties faced by dissimilar functions. Has your firm tried this? Even a short stay in another department (two or three months perhaps) can help managers to adopt wider perspectives.

---

9. If the business has a decentralised structure, how adequate are its procedures for transmitting new and improved methods from one part of the system to others?

5

How to Improve Operational Performance

Introduction

This chapter tells you how to audit and improve the operating efficiency of the major functions of your business. After reading the chapter you should be able to:

- appreciate the key elements of systems thinking and systems analysis and design;
- appraise the firm's procurement, budgeting, marketing and information gathering arrangements;
- understand the meaning of quality management and how quality management systems may be improved.

Systems analysis and systems design

In order to analyse your business systems properly you first need to know exactly what a business system involves. A *system* is a collection of procedures for attaining a tactical objective. *Procedures* are sub-routines for completing particular tasks. Hence, to audit a system you need to examine the adequacy and efficiency of each of its separate procedures. Consider, for instance, the payroll system of a medium-sized firm. This contains procedures for (1) collecting data on wage rates, overtime worked, PAYE tax codes and National Insurance particulars, and (2) converting all these into payslips and monetary transfers into employees' banks. Management's task is to design, install and administer an integrated set of working methods for achieving this aim efficiently. Hence, management has to assemble documents, equipment and people, prepare operating instructions, and organise the interactions of all these elements to ensure that workers actually get paid.

Checkpoint

Do you think of your company's systems in these analytical terms? Developing a logical and diagnostic approach to business systems is the essential first step towards improving the operational performance of the firm. If you have read previous chapters you are already some way towards this objective. Chapter 2 told you how to define your company's mission and strategic objectives; Chapter 3 advised how to analyse the organisational structure of the firm: next you must compartmentalise the various functional parts of the company rationally and appraise their effectiveness.

The basic systems of a typical business (marketing, budgeting, logistics, etc) are examined separately below. Initially, however, it is useful to discuss the general characteristics that any business system needs to possess.

Designing a system

Your first task is to list and describe briefly all the information requirements and outputs of the relevant function. A stock control system, for instance, requires data on stock issues, receipts of supplies, delivery lead times, etc. It then generates information on stock shortages, holding and acquisition costs, and replenishment dates for various inventories. These facts in turn constitute inputs to the firm's overall procurement system, which now adds further information on suppliers' names and addresses, prices, the characteristics of particular materials, and so on.

Adviceline

The best way to decide what should go into a system is to define exactly what you want to get out of it. Specify the outputs (order forms, invoices, production schedules or whatever) required from the system and then work back through all the stages necessary to produce these outcomes. In doing this you will almost certainly identify sub-routines within the wider scheme. For example, particular quality control procedures (testing of samples of output, inspection arrangements, adjustment of tolerances, etc) all contribute to the firm's overall production system.

Unfortunately, sub-routines sometimes continue even though their contributions to a wider system have long since ceased. Thus, for instance, a firm might install an integrated accounting system whereby the recording of each sale causes the system automatically to issue instructions to release an item from stock, to place an order with a supplier (for the replenishment of the firm's own inventory of the item), to print an invoice and then

---

despatch the item to the customer. Yet the firm may continue to operate warehousing and stock control procedures and maintain sales data records based on the needs of a previous system quite independent of the new integrated scheme. Accordingly, for each sub-routine you identify ask yourself:

- its purpose and longer-term objectives;
- how much it costs and whether it could be done more cheaply using alternative methods;
- whether it requires staff training and, if so, whether the work could be rearranged to make training unnecessary;
- whether it creates any duplicated activity and, if so, how this might be removed;
- how easily it can be modified to satisfy anticipated future needs.

The procurement system

The purpose of this system is to obtain the supplies of materials, components, equipment, stationery, etc that the company requires in order to fulfil its mission.

Adviceline

In a small firm, avoid the temptation of putting the person responsible for marketing in charge of purchasing as well. Managements sometimes justify this on the grounds that people who are good at selling should also be able to buy, since they will recognise all the marketing tricks and techniques that external suppliers are likely to use.

In fact, many important aspects of purchasing do not figure at all in the marketing manager's role. True, a marketing specialist will know how to negotiate discounts on bulk purchases; how to avoid being influenced by misleading advertising; how to handle disputes relating to trade descriptions, fitness for intended use, weights and measures, etc, but such experience is no use for devising goods inward inspection and control procedures, the scheduling of inventory replenishments, establishing mechanisms for continuous assessment of the cheapest sources of supply and certain other purchasing activities

Organising the procurement system
Procurement systems may be centralised or decentralised. With a centralised system, one or more people are totally responsible for

buying *all* the firm's inputs. Decentralised methods, conversely, require each unit of the business (department, division, section, subsidiary or whatever) to obtain its own supplies.

Adviceline

In my experience, centralised systems usually work better, even in small businesses where the purchasing manager is not fully engaged in the purchasing function all the time. Centralised procedures allow high-discount bulk buying (individual departments that purchase small amounts of the same item pay top prices), and the purchasing manager becomes expert in product/ quality characteristics, supply sources, delivery periods, etc. There is standardised documentation (order forms and so on) and close liaison with supplying firms and user departments.

A full-time buyer may not have the detailed technical knowledge of certain input materials possessed by departmental specialists, but this may actually help rather than damage the situation, because the buyer will not be tempted to purchase unnecessarily high quality (and expensive) supplies for simple jobs that could use lower quality materials.

Functions of inputs

Insist that staff analyse the *function* of each item they wish to buy. An input's functions are the characteristics that make it work properly (eg, lift a weight, calculate numbers, protect a product). Ask the question, 'what is this item intended to do?' and then ask 'what is the cheapest way of achieving this objective?'

--- *Checkpoint* ---

When did your company last consider the possibility of producing internally some of the items it purchases from outside, and vice versa? Making your own components means that you control their quality and design, and no external profit margins are involved. However, an outside supplier may enjoy large economies of scale in producing the item and thus be able to supply it far cheaper than you could manufacture it yourself. Check this out periodically.

Adviceline

Make purchasing managers fully accountable for their work, set cost cutting targets, and regularly appraise the performance of purchasing staff. This encourages them to establish logical criteria upon which to base purchasing decisions, to behave rationally, and not to respond to outside salespeople's emotive appeals. Specifically, appraise buyers against their abilities to:

- obtain discounts from suppliers;
- purchase on credit;
- secure extensive after-sales service and support facilities;
- guarantee continuity of supply of inputs;
- impose strict quality standards on suppliers;
- persuade suppliers to alter their outputs to correspond to your company's particular requirements.

Checkpoint

Do you purchase on an *ad hoc* basis or through long-term contracts? Whichever method you use, have you considered the alternative? *Ad hoc* methods enable the firm to obtain quotations for each order, whereas long-term contracts usually offer substantial discounts and enable the purchasing firm to carry minimal stocks (items are delivered from the supplier's warehouse as required so that stockholding costs are passed back to the supplying firm).

Purchase of capital equipment

The issues here are (1) who is to be responsible for recommending and authorising capital expenditures (users of plant and equipment, accountants, or other senior managers), and (2) what procedures are needed for controlling capital spending.

Adviceline

If senior managers insist on authorising *all* capital expenditures, make sure that these same managers assume responsibility for the chaos that ensues when worn-out plant and equipment are not replaced. Often, capital spending decisions are taken by a committee, which procrastinates and fails to resolve important issues. Then the members of the committee hide behind the doctrine of collective responsibility when things go wrong. The chair of such a committee should be *personally* accountable for its decisions.

Budgets

Budgeting is without doubt the commonest and most popular technique for controlling expenditure within businesses. It provides a basis for appraising individual and departmental performances, and forces managers to think hard about their resource needs. Budgets impose financial discipline: spendthrift departments can be identified and penalised; for example, by reducing their allocations in the next financial year. However, budgetary control has problems as well as benefits.

(a) Cost consciousness, essential for effective budgeting, can go too far – causing managers to cut costs by unreasonable amounts. Managers who keep well within their budgets earn the approval of seniors. Hence, some managers regard cutting costs as more important than implementation of the measures necessary to improve performance.

Adviceline

If this is a problem in your business consider adopting a 'flexible' budgeting system, ie one which relates the amounts allocated to various sections to appropriate performance indices. Production expenditure budgets, for example, might be determined by current values of sales. Hence it is assumed that increasing sales will require additional resources to sustain and continue the expansion.

Another approach to flexible budgeting is the simultaneous specification of not one but several different budgets for the same department or activity. The budget actually applied will depend on the particular circumstances prevailing at the moment of implementation. Here, the firm recognises the impossibility of foreseeing all future circumstances and so makes allowances for several contingencies.

(b) Some budgets are overspent, others underspent, so that a mechanism is necessary for transferring unused balances to areas which require extra funds.
(c) Budgets can hide inefficiencies. Once a budget has been allocated the manager in charge may seek to spend the entire amount even though, objectively, not all the funds are needed. Naturally, managers tend to use fully all the resources at their command. Wasteful expenditure may occur simply to exhaust outstanding balances.
(d) It is difficult to distinguish between a budget which has been exceeded because of genuine additional spending needs and one exceeded through administrative incompetence. Indeed, unscrupulous individuals may deliberately overspend in order to have their allocations increased in the next period.

Adviceline

The last three problems might perhaps be overcome by moving on to a 'zero-base' budgeting system whereby there is no presumption whatsoever that the amount given in this budgetary period will be repeated. Indeed, each departmental budget is initially set at zero, assuming thereby that no funds will be made available at all. Hence, heads of department must argue for new allocations at the start of *each* period. Managers are forced to review periodically their plans and working methods and are thus encouraged to identify high-cost activities.

A further approach is to use comparisons of actual and budgeted monthly expenditures to compile 'continuous' budgets whereby the monthly budget for a calendar month one year ahead is based on last month's experience. For example, if February's budget is overspent this year, on 28 February a new and higher budget is set for February next year. This saves the time, cost and inconvenience associated with annual budget meetings, negotiations, forecasting systems, etc.

The management information system

An effective management information system (MIS) enables your company to:

- monitor costs and revenues;
- forecast certain events likely to affect the business;
- identify possibilities for improving efficiency and for introducing profitable new products and entering new markets;
- search the wider business environment for developments of interest to the firm.

It provides the information necessary for day-to-day control (ratios of stock to output, profit to working capital, etc) and, most important, it generates data on changes in the long-term efficiency of your various operations. Hence, you can determine whether you need to abandon current activities in favour of alternative types of work.

Strategic information

Strategic informational requirements include data on key business ratios (return on capital employed, ratios of debt to equity capital, interest payable on borrowed money, etc), on current trends in external capital markets, the firm's liquidity position, aggregate cash flow forecasts, market research data, and so on. The system should monitor rates of return achieved on specific investment projects and compare these with the returns initially predicted.

A key MIS function is to highlight potential problems with debtors and suppliers. Your system should be capable of answering the following questions:

- What is the average delay between delivery of goods or the performance of a service and the issue of invoices?
- How quickly do customers settle their accounts?
- What are the effects of offering discounts for prompt payment?
- What is the ratio of creditors to purchasers?
- How long on average do suppliers take to deliver goods?
- To what extent can payments to suppliers be delayed?

Further desirable outputs from an MIS are information on working capital, ratios of work in progress to production, and the causes of machine breakdown and other interruptions to production.

Adviceline

Appraise your MIS under three headings: **when** information is transmitted, **how** it is sent, and to **whom** it goes.

When information is transmitted

Decide which facts need to be reported instantly, and which can wait until the end of the week, month, etc, before they are made known. Note how flows of information among colleagues of equal rank may be interrupted if certain individuals deliberately conceal information or – through incompetence – do not pass it on. Identify the possible sources of difficulty in your firm.

How information is sent

Data needs to be summarised in a form that enables its fast and accurate evaluation prior to taking decisions. Information should flow vertically through the enterprise from its top to its bottom via channels illustrated in the firm's organisation chart. Often, information 'bottlenecks' occur at supervisory and middle management levels since supervisors and middle managers not only receive information from above (and have to decide whether to act on it) but also collect feedback from lower levels. If a manager fails to act on information received the company's chain of command is broken: policies are not implemented; feedback on the success or failure of policies is not transmitted to higher authority.

To whom information goes

Unfortunately, relevant information may not reach the right

---

people. Managers commonly assume that colleagues and subordinates have been informed of particular facts when, actually, they have not. Transmission of every piece of information that may be relevant to an individual is not feasible; otherwise the firm would devote all its time, energy and resources to transmitting messages, most of which were of little practical use. Thus, choices have to be made and dangers exist that the wrong people will receive information.

Thus great care is needed when deciding to whom information should be transmitted. The key criterion is that data be sent to where it is of greatest use in taking decisions.

The marketing audit

A marketing audit should cover:

- the effectiveness of advertising;
- responsiveness of sales to price changes;
- behaviour of competitors;
- the efficiency of distributors;
- lengths of trading cycles (ie the periods that elapse between making a product and its sale to the final consumer);
- trends in various market segments;
- frequency and causes of stockouts;
- the identification of slow moving items;
- stockholding costs.

Further detailed analyses are necessary in respect of each of the following:

Efficiency of the sales force
It sometimes occurs that a small percentage of a sales force accounts for the great majority of sales. Calculate the percentages of total sales achieved by cumulative percentages of your sales force and analyse the results. Can you identify differences in geographical areas covered, regional consumer tastes, training received by various salespeople, etc, that account for major differences in performance?

Product knowledge of marketing staff
Are sales and other marketing personnel fully up to date in their knowledge of company products? If not, why not? What are the implications for sales of marketing staff not being up to date in this respect?

External marketing communications

The business must regularly review and seek to improve its image. Note how company images impress the employees of firms as well as outsiders. Hence a positive image contributes to employee job satisfaction, to the culture of the enterprise (see Chapter 8) and to general morale as well as to increasing sales.

There is a distinction between a business's 'image' and its 'identity'. The image of the enterprise is the mental impression it creates. This image is produced by the company's identity, which consists of the design of its letterheads, logos, typography of promotional literature, the fascia of its premises, and so on. Outsiders (and employees) base their image of the business on their awareness of its identity and on direct experience of the firm's activities and behaviour. Thus, you should always be concerned that the various aspects of your business's identity (its name, letterheads, etc) are congruent and generate favourable images of innovation, quality, dynamism, reliability, success, or other desirable attributes.

--------------------------- *Checkpoint* ---------------------------

Does your business have a deliberate policy for maintaining and improving its image? If not, you could be losing custom.

How do you think outsiders and employees perceive the enterprise? Images are important for the reasons explained in the next section.

The outward disposition your firm projects will create thoughts about, and feelings towards, the business that will encourage outsiders to behave positively or negatively when dealing with the organisation, without their necessarily being fully aware of why this is so. Accordingly, great care is needed when selecting an image.

Note that techniques for projecting one type of image may not be appropriate for projecting others, and once established an image may be extremely difficult to change. The first important decision is selecting which of the firm's potential activities to emphasise and which to leave out, since the business name, letterheads and other promotional material cannot possibly refer to all potential market opportunities.

--------------------------- *Checkpoint* ---------------------------

To what extent does your business name, logo, etc, indicate the types of work your firm undertakes? Read on for an example of a situation where choice of an appropriate business name is crucial.

To illustrate the importance of this point, consider a small building firm whose target customers (householders) wish to replace some guttering or have other relatively minor repairs completed. Such customers will be put off approaching the business if it has created for itself an image of being concerned mostly with large-scale house extensions or major shopfitting. A business that is technically excellent can fail through having the wrong image. Impressions of ability can be as important for winning orders as actual competence to produce and deliver goods.

Controlling a system

The basic options are as follows:

(a) Set targets and simultaneously specify acceptable deviations from these targets (eg, produce 100 units per hour, plus or minus 10 per cent) and then investigate only the divergences that exceed the allowable deviation. Hence, normal operations are dealt with by junior executives, leaving senior managers free to spend their time on unusual problems and policy issues.
(b) Monitor events continuously and intervene to improve performance wherever possible.

Adviceline

Wherever possible adopt the latter (continuous monitoring) approach, though keep the number of controls to the absolute minimum (too many controls create confusion and lead to the proliferation of marginally useful information). The practice of examining only major deviations from predetermined norms is a left-over from the days when firms did not have computers. Businesses generated so much operational data that it was not physically possible to monitor the data continuously. Thus, information was collected on a day-to-day basis but was analysed periodically (monthly, quarterly, half-yearly). By specifying tolerable deviations from target performance and intervening only if the limits of tolerable deviation were exceeded, management could avoid becoming immersed in trivial issues and instead reserve its time and efforts for unusual or exceptionally demanding problems.

Unfortunately, however, serious problems are attached to this method. First, there are time lags between the moment a problem arises, the moment it is noticed, and when remedial action is implemented. Manufacturing cost data, for example, may be collated and analysed once a month; if a particular production line develops a fault and begins to generate unacceptably high expenses at the start of the month, the situation will not be recognised until the month's end. Then there is a further delay before a report goes to higher management, followed by another lag until corrective action is taken. During these delays high extra costs are being incurred.

The second major problem is that since 'acceptable deviations' from target performance are tolerated without investigation, it is possible for a particular activity to be perpetually above or below standard by a relatively small amount without the fact ever being reported. Hence, minor defects can continue, and overall performance will constantly be lower than could be the case. Equally, the cause of consistently superior performance just below the upper reporting boundary will not be examined; there is no mechanism for isolating the factors contributing to high achievement and applying these factors elsewhere.

Increasingly, firms are computerising their administrative systems, with the result that information on costs, outputs, revenues, and other variables is immediately available and (most important) is incorporated into existing analyses as the data come out. Thus, production lines which begin to produce defectives; labour and materials costs which start to get out of hand; increasing overheads; falling sales, etc, can be identified as they happen so that remedial action can be applied instantly.

— Checkpoint —

Does your business monitor its activities continuously or periodically? Have you considered the costs and benefits of each option? Standard costing and variance analysis is a good example of the periodic approach. Here, predetermined expected values are computed for the costs of anticipated materials usage, labour time, machine expenses, etc, and are then compared with *actual* expenditure on these items. Differences (referred to as 'variances') are reported at pre-specified intervals and analysed to identify sources of inefficiency.

In the past, much time and effort have been devoted to the design and development of standard costing systems. Computerisation, of course, removes the need for such procedures because relevant and up-to-date information then becomes immediately available whenever required and is analysed and presented in whatever format the user wishes.

Surprisingly, some firms computerise their production yet *still* continue to prepare standard costing reports in parallel with the information generated by the computerised system. This wastes time, money and effort and adds nothing to what is known already.

Logistics

Inefficient transport and distribution can spell disaster for the firm. Goods will not be delivered to customers on time; presentation of goods will be inadequate and selling prices will be uncompetitively high.

Adviceline

Begin your appraisal of the firm's distribution system in the final marketplace and work backwards to your premises. Could customer satisfaction be improved through altering the methods through which consumers receive or are offered the goods and, if so, how?

Distribution channels

A distribution channel consists of all the business units involved in getting a product to the final consumer. It could include wholesalers, retailers, franchise outlets, mail order selling or door-to-door sales. The questions you need to ask concerning the efficiency of a distribution system are as follows:

- Does each link in the distribution chain perform a unique function that your firm or some other distribution unit could not undertake more effectively?
- If competitors distribute their output in a manner different from your own, why have they chosen these alternative methods?
- Does the customer expect the product to be instantly available? What are the costs and benefits of increasing/decreasing product availability (remember that simply having an item on a certain retailer's shelf does not necessarily mean it will sell)?
- Can some of your distribution channels be controlled more closely than others and, if so, how important is the ability to exercise stringent control?

Adviceline

Decisions about distribution have far reaching consequences for many aspects of the firm's work. The use of intermediaries (wholesalers, for example) means that you lose control over final selling prices and methods for presenting the product to end consumers. Also, the choice of a particular distribution channel typically involves a long-term commitment to other firms plus financial investments that cannot be easily withdrawn. Considering the great importance of the company's distribution system, the more control you are able to exert the better.

- Do your distribution channels enhance or damage the company's image (see above)?

Checkpoint

Sometimes, companies become locked into unsuitable distribution systems without realising the fact. To ascertain whether this has happened to your business, simply assume the firm has just started up and is looking for the best distribution methods. Which channels would you select and how do these differ from current arrangements?

Quality management systems

Whether yours is a manufacturing or a service business you need an effective system for controlling the quality of your products.

Checkpoint

What do you understand by the term 'quality management'? Do you associate it with statistical quality control?

In fact, quality management is much more than statistical calculations, inspection procedures, and so on. It concerns the *total* supply system and is intimately intertwined with every aspect of the company's operations.

There are two possible approaches to quality management.

1. Check work frequently, specify output requirements in great detail, apply the division of labour and supervise employees closely.
2. *Alternatively*, regard inspection and quality control not as independent functions but as integral and inseparable activities, with production (or other) operatives becoming fully responsible for the quality of their work. In this case, there is no autonomous inspection *per se*, because excellence is taken for granted. Inspections are seen not as a means of improving quality but as an insult to the workers concerned.

The latter approach can be applied to outside suppliers. Instead of constantly inspecting the goods they provide, you assume they will furnish high quality inputs as a matter of course. In return, the supplier is expected to operate a *quality assurance system* (see page 85) and automatically compensate you for any defective output that mistakenly enters your firm.

Adviceline
Workers who manage the quality of their own output save the cost of inspectors and become intimately involved with the quality effort of the organisation as a whole. Inevitably, some defective

---

work will occur, yet its quantity need not exceed that normally experienced when independent inspectors are employed. Note, moreover, how quality levels invariably settle just above the minimum acceptable standards whenever minimal criteria are defined.

Quality assurance

The purpose of quality assurance (QA) is to ensure that goods are delivered on time and are fit for the uses for which they are intended.

--- *Checkpoint* ---

Have you heard of BS 5750 or ISO 9000 (its international equivalent)? If yours is a manufacturing business and you are not familiar with BS 5750 you could soon be headed for difficulties. BS 5750 is a 'quality systems' specification published by the British Standards Institution in 1987. Many government departments, local authorities and big businesses now insist that supplying firms adhere to BS 5750 as a condition for the award of contracts (firms inspected and certificated by the BSI as meeting BS 5750 have their names listed in an HMSO publication). BS 5750 is discussed further on page 86.

QA programmes cover every aspect of the work of the firm, including the motivations (as well as the abilities) of employees, their training, suitability for various tasks, and so on. QA standards (such as BS 5750) require supplying firms to implement definite procedures for ensuring that specific quality environments will be maintained (eg, that tools used on certain jobs are of a particular type, and that only qualified and certificated staff are employed on certain projects).

A QA system, moreover, may invite supplying firms to *improve* as well as merely provide contracted items and initiate alterations in the appearance, design or durability of requisitioned products. The quality of goods involves their fitness for the purpose for which they are intended as well as their physical condition on despatch. Suppliers need, therefore, to know the *purposes* of the articles they are invited to produce and the operational circumstances of their use. Hence, a clear statement of the purpose of the item, leaving technical details (including perhaps the choice of input material) to the discretion of the supplying firm, may have greater long-term value than precise and detailed specifications of weights, sizes, machine tolerances, etc. Often, QA is implemented through checklists issued to various departments asking them to scrutinise their procedures and confirm that certain measures have been undertaken.

BS 5750

The aim of BS 5750 is to provide suppliers with a means of obtaining BSI certificated confirmation that their quality management systems are up to scratch. Customers may then have confidence in the supplying company's ability to deliver goods of a pre-specified quality and to maintain the quality of its output at a consistent level.

To qualify for BS 5750 a supplier has to demonstrate excellence in its design procedures and in its inspection and testing methods. It must also show the means by which customers may (1) verify the supplier's claimed quality systems, (2) check records and other documents relating to procedures, and (3) confirm the nature and extent of quality related training given to the supplier's staff. Examples of particular requirements are as follows:

- The firm must produce a quality assurance manual with written procedures detailing:
  - internal allocations of responsibility for various aspects of quality;
  - quality control procedures, methods and work instructions;
  - testing, inspection and audit programmes.
- Staff responsible for verifying quality management procedures must be (demonstrably) independent of other functions.
- Effective control over the quality of output of sub-contractors must be guaranteed.
- Design staff must possess appropriate qualifications.
- The firm must ensure that proper testing equipment is used.
- The firm must ensure that its handling, storing and packaging procedures prevent damage to, or the deterioration of, goods.
- Open access to customers' representatives must be provided, and customers must be given all the inspection and other facilities necessary to verify the supplier's quality procedures.

Need to avoid short-term gimmicks

You may have heard mention of 'quality circles' as a means of quality control. Quality circles were the management 'flavour of the month' for a short while, but in fact very few of the circles set up (often with government funding) during recent years have actually survived.

A quality circle is a departmental discussion group that meets regularly to consider, analyse, investigate and resolve production and quality problems. The group is trained in problem-solving techniques and, most important, is given resources and (limited) authority to implement decisions. Circle leadership may be assumed by an existing departmental supervisor, or by someone directly elected from the group. Circles normally concentrate on mundane practical (rather than organisational) problems and solve them using ideas and methods developed by the workers themselves.

Although they may appear successful in the short run, they usually fail in the longer term. Morale improves initially as workers become involved (often for the first time) in decision-taking, and as participants are brought together to discuss quality and productivity issues. Workers begin to take an interest in company affairs and to apply their personal knowledge, skills and experiences to the solution of quality problems. Since circle decisions are taken by those responsible for their implementation, they are almost certain to be carried out.

Eventually, however, apathy sets in as employees begin to feel they are undertaking (unpaid) extra duties, the benefits of which will accrue entirely to the firm and not to circle members. Improved performances may not be adequately rewarded and frustrations may arise from the circle's inability to solve problems, the sources of which are beyond its control. Antagonisms develop between circle leaders and other managers about how particular difficulties should be overcome and over the extent of the resources and executive authority the circle should command. The circle acquires experience of participative decision-making and may wish to apply this to other areas of the organisation's work (industrial relations or welfare, for example), even though management may oppose employee participation apart from quality circles. Members then regard the circle's terms of reference as unduly restrictive and feel that their efforts are being thwarted by higher management or others outside the group. Attendance at circle meetings falls and meetings themselves are held less frequently. The circle has then effectively collapsed.

Adviceline

What is really needed is a genuine concern for quality throughout the entire organisation, including top management as well as shop-floor operatives. Too often, the establishment of a quality circle is a management's first-ever attempt at employee participation, so that it has no experience of the difficulties that arise from participative techniques. Too often, circles are established as *ad hoc* devices for improving quality and departmental efficiency rather than as genuine long-term attempts to alter management style.

So long as operatives are assumed to be potentially incompetent, producing output that needs regular independent inspection, there are few prospects of improving the quality of output. Negative attitudes towards employees invariably fulfil themselves; treat people as incompetent and they will soon begin to behave incompetently. Concern for quality must be subsumed into the cultural infrastructure of the firm, and not regarded as a special or unusual function.

Job security for employees' single status (see Chapter 6), fair and increasing rewards, genuine participation in decision-making, respect from superiors, teamwork, regular performance appraisal and salary reviews – such are the instruments that create working environments in which employees can reasonably be expected to take a lasting pride in the quality of their work.

6
Leading the Business

Introduction

Previous chapters have suggested measures for determining what exactly your business should do and for devising organisational structures and working methods for achieving objectives. Precisely *how* targets are achieved depends on the mode of leadership adopted by the management of the company.

Management must consciously choose an approach to leadership that will maximise the firm's efficiency and help it to fulfil its mission.

After reading this chapter you will be able to:

- identify contrasting approaches to the leadership of organisations and know the advantages and drawbacks of each of these;
- develop your personal sensitivity to the difficulties experienced by employees in their jobs;
- appreciate the implications of single status for the work of the firm;
- establish a system for setting targets for everyone in the business.

There are several approaches to leadership within companies. The most common are as follows.

1. The participative approach

The major features of this approach are as follows:

- There is much communication between bosses and their

subordinates. The former know a lot about the latter (background, lifestyle, abilities, aspirations, family circumstances, etc) and they frequently meet to discuss work.

- Bosses consult with subordinates before taking important decisions. Targets are set only after a discussion between boss and workers.
- Wherever possible, subordinates are left to achieve targets as they please, using their own methods.
- Employees are invited to participate in forward planning and are encouraged to innovate and suggest new ideas.

Adviceline

Lazy managers sometimes abdicate important responsibilities under the pretext of adopting participative, democratic approaches to leadership. Subordinates are given unreasonably demanding assignments and then left completely alone to take the difficult decisions necessary for their completion. Unfortunately, subordinates may be neither trained nor competent to take such decisions and the boss may not have given them all the information, resources and authority required.

Delegation of work and authority must be carefully planned and (whenever possible) integrated into wider staff development programmes. (See Chapter 7 for further details.)

Advantages of employee participation

The advantages of participative management relate to (1) the firm's use of its workers' knowledge, skills and experience, (2) the stimulation of effort and initiative, (3) greater job satisfaction and increased morale throughout the organisation. On the other hand:

- employees sometimes lack the desire and/or the ability to become involved in management decisions, actually preferring to be told what to do;
- decision-taking may be extremely slow;
- ambiguities may arise about who should do what;
- involving junior employees in *operational* decisions, while excluding them from all *major* decision-taking, could lead to great resentment in the longer term.

--- *Checkpoint* ---

Mission statements of US corporations invariably contain a general commitment to participative management style. Here are some examples.

'We assume our employees want to understand the purpose of their work and of the organisation and want a strong hand in determining what to do and how to do it.'
'We shall exercise the maximum concern for the individual worker and will respect his or her commitment and judgement.'
'We are committed to providing a challenging work environment.'
'We shall ensure that two-way communication is maintained and will provide a climate and resources to enable all our employees to develop and to be excellent in their work.'

UK businesses seem far less inclined to endorse participative management. Why do you think this is the case?

2. Authoritarianism

You have to recognise (1) that certain types of work simply *cannot* be made interesting and (2) that some workers are seemingly immune to any and all attempts to stimulate their commitment and interest. You can lead a horse to water, but you cannot make it drink!

Adviceline

Boredom may be caused by continuous repetition of a simple task or by the social environment in which work is undertaken. Thus, although a job may be interesting, the worker may still feel bored through the social isolation that the work involves. Equally, a job may be trivial and repetitious, yet not create boredom because the worker is able to communicate with others and find distractions from his or her mundane duties. Complicated tasks require concentration. Workers performing complex jobs typically become absorbed by them and do not experience boredom. Thus, the more complicated you can make a job (within reason and the worker's capacity to perform it satisfactorily), the better it may be for all concerned.

Authoritarian approaches may be appropriate for situations where employees lack motivation, show little concern for their work and make no attempt to communicate with colleagues or supervisors. Such environments are common where physical working conditions are unpleasant, where the tasks undertaken are trivial and mundane, and where wages are low.

You should, of course, examine these situations to see whether employees' jobs can be made more interesting. This might be possible through:

- frequent job rotation so that workers experience a variety of social circumstances while completing their work;
- extending the range of the employees' duties and responsibilities;
- allocating the workers more difficult (and hence challenging) tasks.

Only then should authoritarian approaches be considered.

Characteristics of the authoritarian approach

Authoritarianism has the following characteristics:

- Senior management takes all significant decisions, which are imposed without comment or discussion.
- Employees are given precise and detailed instructions about how to undertake their work.
- Interpersonal relations are highly formal;
- Subordinates are strictly controlled.

Authoritarian styles may be either (1) detached and impersonal or (2) paternalistic. The latter still involve tight supervision, but managers consciously attempt to capture the respect and allegiance of subordinates. Thus, senior managers bestow favours on obedient and hardworking employees, and some dissent is tolerated (though it is never condoned). The authoritarian approach has a number of disadvantages.

(a) It stifles employees' initiative.
(b) Staff are not allowed to develop to their full potential.
(c) If senior managers are away (holidays, illness, etc) this often means that important work is not completed.

Adviceline

Authoritarianism is usually frowned upon in academic management studies literature. Yet it has advantages as well as drawbacks, including the following:

- There is a high probability that tasks will actually be completed, on time and to a predetermined standard.
- Situations and relationships are clearly defined.
- Solutions to problems are imposed rather than (ineffectively) debated.
- The firm actively seeks positive ways of doing new things rather than merely reacting to events.
- There is efficient co-ordination of work (see Chapter 3).
- Subordinates are directed and thus *helped* towards achieving their targets.
- Management becomes the focal point of the enterprise.

Thus, you ought not to dismiss authoritarianism out of hand.

---

3. The entrepreneurial approach

Here, managers (and to some extent other workers) are encouraged – indeed expected – independently to seek fresh opportunities for improved performance. Managers may not be the owners of the firm, but are instructed to behave *as if* this were the case. Accordingly, when taking any decision a manager should ask him or herself the simple question, 'What would I do if it was my own personal money that I had to spend on this project?', and proceed accordingly. Possession of entrepreneurial attitudes by paid employees (rather than the owners) of a business is sometimes referred to as 'intrapreneurship'. This may be encouraged in the following ways:

- Giving managers personal budgets and then leaving them to achieve objectives exactly as they see fit.
- Establishing roving 'action squads' whose function is to roam around the organisation seeking fresh ways of improving efficiency, locating lucrative new markets, finding cost-cutting opportunities, etc. Each action squad is self-contained and a cost/profit centre in its own right, with the authority to intervene in any aspect of the business. Heads of department may be seconded to action squads for short periods in order (1) to stimulate their entrepreneurial attitudes and (2) to develop their overall awareness of the work of the firm.
- Treating each department as an independent self-financing enterprise, that 'buys in' inputs and services from other parts of the business, adds value to inputs and then 'sells' the resulting output to other sections of the organisation.
- For multi-product firms, creating departments to oversee the supply of just one product and nothing else. Staff in the department control all activities associated with the product including the purchase of raw materials, manufacture (where appropriate), administration, advertising, and the sale and distribution of the final goods. Thus, employees are forced to think *as if* they were running a separate business rather than a section of a firm.

Adviceline

Entrepreneurial approaches inevitably involve attitudes towards risk. If you want people to behave entrepreneurially you have to reward their willingness to assume risk and to take responsibility for decisions.

There will, of course, be failures as well as successes, and in consequence a relatively high turnover of managerial staff. Suppose that within such a system there were no penalties for

---

non-achievement of targets. The scheme would lose its credibility and the organisation would eventually collapse as managers took increasingly risky and inappropriate decisions, lackadaisically and without fear of adverse consequences should things go wrong.

Checkpoint

Entrepreneurship within organisations is a state of mind as well as a method of controlling operations. Some of the characteristics of an entrepreneurial attitude are as follows:

(a) perseverance and determination, manifest in willingness to work extremely hard;
(b) willingness to take risks, though only after a careful investigation of the likelihood of success;
(c) an intuitive understanding of the operation of the marketplace, particularly in relation to the identification of new market opportunities;
(d) unwillingness to be bound by convention, plus a dislike of bureaucracy and restrictive rules;
(e) emotional commitment to the organisation.

Using these criteria, how many of your colleagues would you describe as having entrepreneurial approaches? If the answer is, 'not many', do you believe the introduction of measures to encourage entrepreneurial attitudes would significantly improve the performances of the least entrepreneurial of the staff?

4. Situational management

This is a reactive management style whereby, instead of applying a single approach regardless of circumstances, the firm adapts its style to correspond to the needs of each particular situation.

Adviceline

Superficially, this appears to be the best and obviously sensible method. All approaches have their strengths and weaknesses, and different styles may or may not be appropriate depending on the environments in which decisions are made. Autocratic styles may be suitable when quick and/or unpopular decisions are necessary; democratic approaches may be better when employees' expert knowledge, initiative and experiences are required. Participative leadership may stimulate workers' interest and motivation; but disagreements can arise and decision-making processes become extremely slow. Clearly, therefore, differing work situations call for different management styles.

There are, however, problems attached to the situational approach.

(a) Employees may find management's behaviour confused, contradictory and inconsistent. Practical application of the approach requires management to alter its style from one situation to the next and from one group of workers to another. Management may choose to be autocratic today and democratic tomorrow, depending on circumstances. Employees (and others) thus need to predict how management is likely to behave in any given situation.

(b) Individual managers may not possess the skill or maturity necessary to vary their approaches in the manner suggested, especially if they have not been trained in the techniques of situational leadership.

(c) It may be entirely appropriate to apply certain basic principles to all managerial work regardless of circumstances, especially where human relations and/or employee welfare are concerned.

Applying the situational approach

To be good at situational management you have to be capable of recognising the factors that distinguish one type of situation from others. Such factors include:

- whether employees' work is routine or varied, boring or interesting;
- the background, abilities and motivation of employees;
- the duration of the project (workers may be happy to accept a directive, autocratic style in the short but not in the longer term);
- how much employees know about their work, and their general levels of commitment and competence.

Then you must match your style to the situation and – where this is possible – control the work environment to your advantage; for example, by making employees' jobs more or less detailed or by extending or reducing the discretion allowed to subordinates over how they complete assignments.

Checkpoint

List at least six words or phrases to describe the style of management applied in your company.

A personal observation

The more I see of large US and British organisations, the more aware I become of the enormous cultural gap that seems to exist between the best American companies and their UK counterparts. Too many large British businesses, I believe, are run on 'traditional', rigid and hierarchical lines with little (if any) direct communication between the top and bottom of the firm. Frequently, senior management is segregated from lower levels of worker both physically and with respect to social background and experience, class, accent, education and general lifetime opportunities as a whole. Relations between high and low are suffocatingly formal; there is much status consciousness and minimal occupational mobility within the firm.

I contrast this with some of the large US companies of which I have experience, where everyone – from the company president down to the most recent recruit – is on first name terms and where all employees speak and dress in a similar way (subject, of course, to occupational necessities). There is a 'shirt sleeve' approach to management, with senior executives becoming intimately involved in day-to-day operations and top people regularly communicating with junior members of staff. Interpersonal relations are informal and there is great emphasis on *teamwork*. Of course, not every big US corporation meets these standards, but the norms of behaviour just described do seem to represent the sort of approach to leadership to which most large US businesses aspire, even if these standards are not actually accomplished.

Improving leadership style

The key to improving leadership style is *sensitivity* on the part of managers, who need to understand subordinates, their work, and their feelings towards the organisation.

Adviceline

'Empathy' means seeing and trying to experience a situation as it is perceived by another person. To empathise with employees means entering and sharing their feelings about work.

You can only empathise with people if you talk to them. When doing this, a good way of testing the extent of your empathy with the other person is for you to interrupt the conversation occasionally and make the comment:

'You feel . . . (now fill in your interpretation of what the person meant by his or her last few statements) . . . *because* . . . (insert your interpretation of his or her *reasons* for feeling that way).

A simple example might be:

'You feel that Maureen let you down badly last week by not

> providing you with the information on outstanding debtors she promised, because she knew it was urgent, she had more than enough time to collect the data, and yet she could not be bothered to make the effort to collate the files.'
>
> This simple device conveys to subordinates your interest in learning about their opinions and confirms your understanding of how they perceive events and issues.
>
> Note, however, that a sensitive manager not only empathises with employees, but also will *act* to remedy problems.

The most immediate and powerful way of causing managers to reassess (and perhaps alter) their management style is to incorporate the effectiveness of their approach to leadership into the appraisal scheme used to measure their performance. Annual or half-yearly appraisals typically constitute a significant input into the assessment of the individual manager's pay and promotion prospects, thus creating direct incentives for the manager to adopt the leadership style most appropriate for the needs of the organisation.

Headings for the evaluation of a person's leadership ability might include the following:

- the successes he or she has achieved in developing subordinates' abilities;
- the capacity to create enthusiasm among the staff;
- loyalty of subordinates;
- frequency and quality of interactions with junior employees, etc.

The weights attached to these criteria in the total assessment of the manager's performance can be increased or decreased according to the desirability of changing the company's existing management style.

— *Checkpoint* —

Do you address all your colleagues and subordinates in the same tone of voice and manner regardless of their sex and occupational status? Do you, for instance, address junior secretarial staff with the same courtesy you would use when speaking to a senior executive? If not, try consciously to be more civil towards low status workers.

Saying 'thanks'

How often do managers within your company openly thank their subordinates for having performed excellent work? There is no doubt that the satisfaction derived from formal recognition of the value of an employee's efforts can greatly motivate the individual. A short memorandum on the lines, 'Thanks for your tremendous effort in winning the XYZ order', or 'Your presentation to last week's divisional committee was really excellent', not only pleases the worker but also lets everyone know that their work is being observed and that exceptionally good (or bad) results will be noted.

The quality of working life
Efficient and sensitive managers know which types of work their subordinates find interesting; which they find boring; and why. Then they try to increase the interesting component of subordinates' jobs.

Adviceline
Consider the job of any one of your immediate subordinates. List the interesting duties (those which carry responsibility and involve much discretion and self-control) that you believe to be attached to the position, and then specify what you consider to be the boring aspects of the job. Now have the subordinate repeat the process, independently and without seeing the lists you have prepared. Compare the results. Are there any differences you find surprising? If so, why?

Having identified the boring aspects of the subordinate's work, see whether you can make the job more varied (eg, by regrouping activities, taking some interesting work away from certain individuals and reallocating it to others, or by allowing the employee greater control over the pace or methods of completing work).

Single status
Single status is seemingly anathema to most large British companies – despite the sensationally successful examples recently set by a number of UK based subsidiaries of Japanese firms. Yet single status (ie workers and their bosses eating in the same canteen, wearing similar clothes, enjoying equal access to superannuation and company welfare benefits, comparable fringe benefits, profit sharing, availability of low-interest loans, etc) can dramatically increase a business's productivity and the morale of its workforce.

In adopting single status, management transmits a strong and clear signal that it values and respects all its employees. The sight of senior directors carrying their own trays in the company canteen, of heads of department having to turn up early in order to guarantee a parking space in the firm's car park, of directors clocking-in alongside all other grades of staff, etc, tells the world that top management is genuinely committed to working as an integral part of a company-wide team and is not concerned with petty status differentials. Indeed, attitudes towards status in general are perhaps the clearest indicator there is of a company's leadership style.

———————————— *Checkpoint* ————————————

Has your company ever considered introducing single status? It has many advantages, including the following:

(a) The process of introducing single status may be accompanied by a productivity agreement to reduce the extent of overtime working (say) or otherwise improving the economic efficiency of the business.
(b) It removes petty yet vexatious differences in individual rewards.
(c) Staff turnover might be reduced.
(d) The firm increases its ability to redeploy workers. (The existence of numerous status differentials makes it difficult to move people into jobs that do not carry the same status privileges as previously.) Thus, single status necessarily encourages the acceptance of change.
(e) Individual employees become more inclined to identify with the company *as a whole* rather than with a particular grade within its status hierarchy.

Note how many contemporary status differentials began in historical circumstances quite different from modern conditions. For example:

- It is no longer the case that white collar staff necessarily earn more than production operatives (as was invariably the case in the 1800s and the early years of this century).
- The terms 'white' and 'blue' collar worker are themselves not *literally* applicable today because (compared to the past) relatively few contemporary manual jobs need be physically dirty. There is no reason in principle why operatives and managers in most modern firms should not dress in a similar manner.
- The availability of mechanical handling devices has removed many previously important distinctions between 'light' and 'heavy' labour.
- A century of public education has created a labour force that, for the most part, is literate and capable of communicating meaningfully with people from other backgrounds and in higher level occupations.
- Many manual jobs that (normally) do not carry 'staff' status (with superannuation, etc) in fact require more skill and longer periods of training than certain non-manual jobs that automatically attract 'staff' benefits.
- The values to the firm of manual and non-manual occupations have narrowed in many areas.
- Nowadays, skills shortages are just as likely in manual as in non-

manual occupations so that it is no longer necessary to offer higher status to non-manual workers as a recruitment incentive.

Adviceline

If you introduce single status to your company, do it comprehensively and with a 'big bang', not partially and gradually. Some firms accept the desirability of single status but then restrict its provision to long-serving manual employees, or to those who carry certain responsibilities, and/or to those in particular occupational categories. Yet within the same firms, non-manual workers continue to achieve staff status automatically. If anything, more rather than less resentment will arise through following this procedure.

Target setting

Few managers today dispute the desirability of 'management by objectives'. The advantages of target setting are numerous. They include:

- the establishment of direct relationships between the organisation's primary goals and individual performances;
- the provision of a rational basis for employee appraisal;
- clarification of management's expectations regarding the activities to be undertaken by each person;
- forced preplanning of work;
- the creation of opportunities for bosses and subordinates to meet, discuss issues, examine the feasibilities of proposed objectives, exchange information, etc;
- motivation of workers.

Target setting methods

The available options are are follows:

(a) Management simply informs individuals of their targets. Subordinates are then invited to comment on the targets set.
(b) Employees propose their own targets and discuss them with their bosses.
(c) Subordinates are given predetermined targets, but then consult their bosses about the best ways of achieving objectives.
(d) Targets are predetermined, but subordinates have total discretion in choosing methods for their attainment.

Adviceline

Select the method which involves the greatest amount of interaction between bosses and subordinates. The meetings at which objectives are established offer (like appraisal interviews) ideal opportunities for discussing a wide range of issues affecting subordinates' work. Individuals meet their bosses in a neutral environment away from the pressure of day-to-day operations, so both parties can 'let their hair down' and properly explore outstanding problems. Moreover, targets *mutually* agreed by boss and subordinate are far more likely to be achieved than targets arbitrarily imposed without consultation.

Hierarchy of objectives

The aim is to integrate company and personal targets into a unified and coherent set of activities. Organisational objectives derive from the company's mission (see Chapter 2), and need to be broken down into lesser targets for divisions, functions, departments, sections and ultimately for individual staff members.

Adviceline

Set targets in three areas:

- for routine operations (meeting a sales target, for instance);
- for developing new activities and/or introducing fresh ideas (eg, initiating and managing new projects such as the inauguration of a system or the launch of a product);
- for innovation, ie finding completely different things that the firm might do (locating a new market opportunity or discovering a new way of reducing costs, for instance).

Rules for setting targets

Any system for setting targets should exhibit the following features:

- Each target must relate to the company's mission.
- Targets should be precise, unambiguous and (if possible) expressed numerically. Generic objectives such as 'increase profits' or 'cut costs' are not acceptable.
- Written records of targets agreed during objective setting interviews should be retained in order to assist subsequent reviews and appraisals of employees' activities.
- Once set, a target should remain for a reasonable period. Targets should not be increased arbitrarily when it becomes obvious that they will be quickly and easily exceeded.

- Sensible criteria must be applied when establishing objectives (numbers should not be pulled out of the air) and the targets established should be reasonably attainable. Otherwise, it becomes impossible for *any* job occupant to achieve its objectives.
- Each major target should be accompanied by an *action plan* listing the resources, facilities and operations necessary for its achievement.
- Targets should relate to the crucial and primary elements of subordinates' jobs and not to trivial matters.

Adviceline

It is easier to determine specific targets for members of a department if the central aim of the department (which results from its intended contribution to the achievement of the company's mission) is clarified and broadcast to all departmental employees. The central aim is a statement of the reason for the department's existence. Without a clear central aim it is impossible to determine precisely the tasks that must be done and the resources and authority necessary for their successful completion. If a department head cannot specify what he or she expects the department to achieve, it becomes extremely difficult to define meaningful targets for subordinates.

CHECKLIST

1. Who within the organisation shows most interest in developing new strategies: line managers, senior directors, recent entrants to the firm, or those with the greatest experience? How do you account for differences in level of interest?
2. Are strategic alternatives regularly, openly and *voluntarily* discussed at all levels of the company's management? If not, why are employees reluctant or unable to talk about strategic issues?
3. How frequently does senior management change its priorities? Are the reasons for such alterations explained to staff and, if so, are they accompanied by apologies for the inconvenience caused by the changes?
4. Does there exist within the organisation an unofficial communication system that circumvents official channels?

Adviceline

A common indication of inappropriate management style is the emergence within companies of informal 'shadow' organisation and communication systems. These tend to arise in the following circumstances:

- when the objectives of individuals conflict with the aims of the business, especially where the allocation of resources (including money for wage increases) is involved;
- if employees do not wholeheartedly support the mission and philosophy of the enterprise;
- if staff are not fully aware of the firm's core objectives;
- when routine departmental decisions are regularly overruled by higher authority – this causes junior managers to conceal many of their activities from superiors, hence creating an unofficial authority system within the business;
- where few facilities exist for formal interdepartmental communication.

Unofficial communication channels (or 'grapevines' as they are often called) misrepresent situations, distort reality, exaggerate issues, and become a vehicle for carrying unpleasant and deceitful rumours. Also, the individuals who disseminate information through unofficial channels sometimes assume an undeservedly high status in the eyes of fellow workers.

The best way of destroying unofficial communication systems is to present employees with copious amounts of accurate and relevant information. Do *not* be tempted to use unofficial communication channels yourself; for example, for testing likely employee reaction to possible redundancies. Misunderstandings of your true intentions can quickly escalate and make your task more difficult in the longer term.

5. Can you identify direct links between the company's management style and employee motivation? If so, how do these associations operate?
6. Which level of employee within the organisation feels greatest responsibility for achieving its objectives? Why is this?
7. How well do you think the firm's senior managers genuinely understand subordinates' problems? If the answer is 'not very well at all', what can be done to improve the situation?
8. Does more information flow downwards through the organisation than flows upwards? Whichever is the case, what are the implications of your answer for controlling the business?
9. How often do senior managers seek fresh ideas from their subordinates? Should this happen more frequently?
10. Does the top management in your company trust its subordinates? If not, why not, and what must be done to improve senior management's confidence in junior managerial staff?

7

How to Solve Your People Problems

Introduction

People management is far more than hiring, firing and controlling workers. It concerns everything to do with putting together and supervising teams of employees for the purpose of helping the business to fulfil its mission. Accordingly, it involves:

- identification of labour requirements;
- matching the personal aspirations of employees to the needs of the organisation;
- bonding workers to the firm;
- developing and motivating workers;
- managing new patterns of work and employment;
- hiring and firing staff.

Effective personnel policies have enormously beneficial consequences. Staff are keen to further the interests of the organisation, to work together in harmonious groups, to take decisions, and will perceive few (if any) fundamental conflicts of interest between personal and company goals.

─────────────── *Checkpoint* ───────────────
List at least five words or phrases to describe the state of morale within your organisation. (The list might include words such as apathy, enthusiasm, frustration, determination, etc.)

Now go through these words and phrases, scoring each one between minus ten (for those with the most damaging connotations) and plus ten (for the most positive). Is the result less than zero? If it is, what does this tell you about the management of the firm in recent years?

As small firms expand, the complexity of their labour problems generally increases. Contracts of employment have to be drafted; grievance procedures implemented; there is the need for collective bargaining with union representatives, and the operational control of numerous workers becomes difficult. Accordingly, at this point in their development many growing businesses begin to consider establishing separate personnel departments. If your firm is in this position, think very carefully indeed before setting up an autonomous personnel section. Large, clumsy and bureaucratic empires can arise from newly formed personnel departments, with personnel officers becoming more concerned with the latest personnel management fads and fantasies than with the pursuit of the company's mission.

If line managers are properly trained and experienced, they should be quite competent to handle the personnel function. Obviously, special problems requiring detailed knowledge of labour management arise occasionally (eg, the implementation of redundancies against complicated legal and/or industrial relations backgrounds, or the need to design a new job evaluation system, or the need to deal with a summons to appear before an industrial tribunal), but you can always engage an external human resources management consultant to deal with such difficulties.

Teamwork

What really matters is that there is openness, trust and mutual interaction between bosses and their subordinates – with or without the intervention of a separate personnel department. Two-way communication is essential, with everyone knowing exactly what is expected of them by other people.

--- *Checkpoint* ---

If yours is a hierarchical management system, how much direct contact is there between non-sequential levels; for example, between employees in grade 2 and those in grade 4, between grades 3 and 5, etc? Would you expect efficiency to improve following more frequent direct contact between non-sequential levels? If so why, and if not why not?

What is a team?

All teams are working groups, but not every group is a 'team'. What makes a team special is that its members co-operate and *voluntarily* work towards common goals. There is much interaction among participants, who feel extremely upset if other team members are idle or otherwise let them down. In a team, people feel inwardly responsible for promoting group interests and personally accountable for its work. Team members will exchange roles, share assignments, and generally help each other to complete their duties.

Adviceline

Team spirit is obviously desirable within an organisation. To foster team spirit in a section, department, division or other organisational unit, the following rules should be applied:

- The unit manager should conspicuously fight for resources on behalf of the team.
- Group members should not be criticised in front of outsiders.
- The manager should always represent and defend the team against the external world.
- Members must be actively encouraged to suggest new working methods and ideas for group activity, and to solve problems independently.
- The distribution of work and responsibility within the group must be visibly fair, especially if unpleasant or exceptionally demanding duties are involved.
- Work should be organised in such a way that each member has to depend on the efforts of other members – even for people of unequal occupational rank. This will create a unity of purpose within the team.
- Participants must be fully aware of the extent of their individual and collective responsibilities. (Many conflicts arise from petty 'who does what' issues.)
- Work programmes need to be carefully planned, with realistic objectives.

Corporate demographics

What are the age and skills distributions of the company's employees? Beware of the situation where skills essential to the business's survival are concentrated in the hands of just a few ageing workers (who might all retire simultaneously) or in the hands of some other small group of people; the resignation of one or two key people can have devastating consequences.

Adviceline

If you have not already done so, examine the feasibility of maintaining a 'skills inventory' of the talents, experiences and qualifications of all the firm's workers. This will enable you to compare existing human resources with the human resources required for the business to attain its mission, and hence to initiate training and/or recruitment policies aimed at remedying deficiencies. The document will also be useful for drafting a management succession programme.

A problem with skills inventories is, of course, the need to question the staff about their knowledge and special abilities in fields not related to current occupations. Why, for example. should an accounts clerk disclose whether he or she can speak a foreign language, or a production worker reveal competencies in motor maintenance or mathematics?

Employees often resent such queries, perceiving these as irrelevant intrusions into private affairs. It is essential, therefore, to emphasise that the information is being gathered to *help* individual workers – by establishing their suitability for higher level work, by identifying training possibilities, and (most important) by finding alternative jobs they could do if redundancies were threatened.

Checkpoint

What do you understand by the word 'supervision'? Many people think of supervision only in terms of first line management, with 'supervisors' being regarded as a sort of link between management and the shop floor. Yet the *concept* of supervision has far wider implications and involves an extensive variety of management skills: delegation, organisation, co-ordination, liaison with unions, motivation and development of employees, counselling, etc.

Supervision

Effective supervision is the key to successful labour management. The term 'supervision' in this context does *not* mean constant inspection of subordinates' work, issuing detailed instructions and/or breaking work down into simple and narrowly defined tasks. Rather, it concerns the day-to-day management of all the firm's operational systems (see Chapter 5) at the tactical level using those interpersonal skills that enable managers to communicate effectively, influence and lead others, plan, co-ordinate and control. Most of all, it requires the ability to create and sustain teams (see page 105).

Practical supervision

Many of the best supervisors I know are not conscious of their exceptional supervisory abilities. Rather, they appear to know *instinctively* how best to direct and monitor other people's work. Nevertheless, all good supervisors seem to adopt a similar approach to their supervisory duties. This approach includes the following elements:

1. Confronted with any problem or situation they immediately specify **rules and procedures** to sort it out. They recognise the need to impose order, to clarify, classify, categorise and determine what exactly has to happen if an objective is to be achieved. Accordingly, they ensure that they *understand* the true nature of the difficulties they confront; they search for similar problems and situations previously solved or experienced, and they break down complicated issues into small and manageable components.

2. They set (reasonable) **targets** for subordinates, relate these targets to the achievement of wider objectives, and suggest to subordinates practical ways in which their targets may be attained.

3. Subordinates' work is closely **monitored** though not in obstructive or overbearing ways. Each subordinate knows that his or her work is being appraised, and that the assessment system used has a coherent structure: interviews, checklists, reports, etc.

4. Excellent work completed by subordinates is openly congratulated; sub-standard work is not tolerated. The expectation of high quality work from subordinates is made obvious. Remedial action to correct shoddy work is *always* implemented.

5. They try to make subordinates' jobs interesting; for example, by combining single tasks into a composite whole, allowing workers discretion over working methods, making subordinates personally responsible for quality control, and by allocating challenging duties that stretch workers' abilities.

Adviceline

Targets that stretch workers to their maximum capacities are generally preferable to targets which are easily achieved. A challenging objective gives the employee opportunities to show what he or she is capable of achieving, to acquire experience of higher level work, to apply a variety of skills to their duties, exercise initiative, and generally gain confidence and competence. The achievement of stiff targets necessarily requires the employee to become interested and involved with the business and to seek better methods of completing assignments.

Motivating workers

Do the firm's employees lack ambition and drive? Are they unwilling to initiate activities or suggest new ideas? Several factors contribute to negative attitudes among workers, including:

- senior management's failure to delegate interesting and challenging duties;

- managers not backing up subordinates when things go wrong;
- lack of financial and other incentives;
- resistance to change caused by the .desire to protect personal interests;
- lack of accountability and inadequate appraisal.

In some firms (usually those with large and bureaucratic organisations) workers are not given targets; there is no employee evaluation and minimal accountability. These are the businesses that eventually fail. Accountability and appraisal help to ensure that targets are actually met, and *themselves* generate enthusiasm and positive attitudes. One firm I know (a public relations consultancy) operates the following system for executive motivation.

- Staff arrive for work at around 9.00 am. At 9.15 they meet for ten or fifteen minutes in groups of four to discuss targets for the day and to establish priorities. Each group is supervised by a manager who outranks other participants.
- During the day each executive places copies of key letters and memoranda that he or she has written, reports prepared, comments on other people's reports and letters, notes on new ideas, and so on, into a 'night box' that is sent to his or her supervisor at about 4.30 pm. The supervisor quickly examines these night boxes, making brief notes on the documents they contain.
- There is a short team meeting at 5.00 pm to highlight major problems or opportunities for new business that have arisen during the day. Staff think about these matters overnight.
- Issues arising from the previous afternoon's meeting or from team members' night boxes are raised at the 9.15 meeting the following day.
- The cycle is repeated weekly on a more general level among group supervisors who meet on Mondays to plan and co-ordinate the week's activities, and on Fridays to review the week's work.

There is much effort and creativity in this company. Staff constantly strive to excel and to initiate new ideas. A progressive and enthusiastic atmosphere pervades the organisation.

Problem people
Businesses cannot afford lazy workers; drastic and immediate measures are necessary whenever morale begins to fall. Policies could include:

- strict supervision in the immediate short term;
- putting staff on to a payments-by-results basis (or at least making future pay rises contingent upon the achievement of targets if existing contracts of employment prohibit payment by results);

- rapid job rotation coupled with the allocation to indolent workers of lots of extra jobs;
- conspicuously promoting employees who are more enthusiastic than the rest;
- short sharp shocks, disciplinary interviews, formal warnings and the dismissal of staff whose work does not improve.

Treating staff as professionals

Much has been said and written about how professionally qualified employees (accountants, lawyers, researchers, specialist engineers, and so on) should be controlled. Traditionally, only managers performing 'service' roles (the company secretary or personnel officer, for example) have been regarded as 'professional' workers. You might wish, however, to consider treating *all* managers, including line managers who belong to no professional organisation, as 'professionals'. In practice, this means:

- assuming as a matter of course that junior managers are competent to exercise discretion in their work and, in consequence, recognising each manager's right to take decisions;
- involving managers in the appraisal of their peers as well as their subordinates;
- making managers *personally* responsible for decisions;
- wide spans of control (see Chapter 4).

Differential payments systems

These are schemes whereby employees' remunerations increase by *extremely* large amounts for improvements in performance at high levels of efficiency, but by low amounts if performance is poor. The relation between reward and achievement is sketched in Figure 7.1.

Such systems can greatly motivate workers through presenting them with the possibility of really high earnings. The cost of the scheme is, of course, financed by the superior performance it creates. Nevertheless, serious difficulties can emerge, illustrated perhaps by the experience of a UK computer firm for which I once completed a consultancy assignment.

The company paid its travelling salespeople in the manner previously outlined. Staff were hardworking and, through the scheme, received a good level of income. The firm then introduced a new type of computer which sold extremely well. Not only was it attractive to existing outlets but it was adopted by a number of schools and colleges for use in classrooms. Inevitably, therefore, parents began asking retail computer stores for information about the new machine and this – in conjunction with the conventional advertising and special promotions attached to the launch of the new product – created a huge demand. Whereas in the

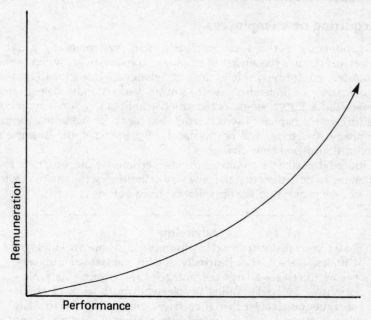

Figure 7.1

past salespeople were taking orders for perhaps three or four machines at a time, they now sold 50 or 60 (sometimes hundreds) to each outlet.

Salespeople's incomes rocketed. They increased their earnings by at least 300 per cent (the best receiving far more than the highest paid executives in the firm). This distorted salary differentials throughout the organisation and other employees bitterly resented the salespeople's gigantic pay packets. Also, the extra salary costs were a substantial financial burden on the firm since, obviously, it was not necessary to pay the current levels of wages to attract and retain reasonable sales staff. Different salespeople could be hired on new contracts at a fraction of the cost.

Sensing that the days of the differential bonus scheme were numbered the salesforce (sensibly from their point of view) colluded to ensure that they could take a sizeable proportion of the firm's customers away with them if they were forced to leave the business. Eventually an across-the-board salary cut was negotiated, with the sales staff being put on to a high time based wage system. In consequence, the salespeople lost their incentive to secure large orders and aggregate sales declined, especially following the introduction by competitors of alternative new machines. The firm eventually collapsed.

Acquiring new employees

Organisations, perhaps unconsciously, may systematically attract, select and retain a certain *type* of employee: conservative, cavalier, well-educated, conformist, intellectual, or whatever. Unfortunately, the aggregation of individuals with similar backgrounds, beliefs and personalities into a single organisational unit can create a business culture (see Chapter 8) which, while excellent for achieving *current* company objectives, will be hopelessly inadequate if the business's circumstances suddenly change.

Indeed, the climate within a business becomes so inappropriate for attaining its objectives that the only way of improving the situation is to inject new people into the organisation from outside.

Adviceline

If, alas, you must recruit externally in order to improve employee attitudes, do so wholeheartedly and in substantial numbers, seeking to replace a large percentage of the existing staff. New entrants – especially young people who must work alongside colleagues much older than themselves – need to be able to relate to each other as well as to existing personnel. The fresh and energetic attitudes of recent recruits need to permeate the business.

Apathy and inertia among current employees must not be allowed to stifle the initiative of the new intake. It is essential, therefore, that senior management openly endorse (and reward) the recruits' progressive attitudes.

Promotion

Apart from improvements in pay and conditions of work, the most immediate incentive available to an employee is the possibility of promotion. If the firm has trained its staff adequately and ensured that their work experiences are sufficiently wide-ranging, internal promotion should present no problem.

--- *Checkpoint* ---

Are your employees fully aware of the criteria the company uses to determine promotions? When did you last review these criteria?

Adviceline

Whether you should opt for ability related promotion criteria (which accelerate the careers of exceptionally competent workers)

---

or for a seniority based system (ensuring steady progression of all employees) depends on the circumstances of the business. The most important variables to consider when making the choice are the calibre of existing personnel, their attitudes and motivation, and whether certain positions require specialist workers who possess job-specific qualifications. Whichever method you select it should be demonstrably fair, objective and, above all, *consistent*.

The knowledge that promotion is available can improve morale throughout the organisation. Also, interpersonal relationships between managers and subordinates improve, labour turnover falls (since able staff do not need to leave the firm to perform higher level duties) while efficiency should increase through use in senior positions of the accumulated experience of long-serving workers.

Note that there is little risk of the individuals promoted possessing unknown deficiencies, as occurs with externally recruited staff. On the other hand, outsiders can inject fresh ideas and apply new perspectives to existing problems, and external recruits may be of much higher calibre than internal candidates.

Adviceline
Never deny an individual the chance of promotion simply because that person is performing excellently in his or her present job. It is unfair to block an individual's prospects simply because he or she has become indispensable in a certain position. If you do, the employee is likely to leave the firm completely, so his or her talents are then lost completely.

Need for qualitative changes
A change in the company's mission may call for *qualitative* as well as quantitative variations in the structure of its workforce. In particular, the skills and attitudes needed to manage a variegated strategic business unit (see Chapter 4), a flexible workforce (see page 114); a networking system (see Chapter 4), or some other unorthodox organisational system may be quite different from those the company previously required.

Adviceline
When recruiting new staff, look for candidates with positive attitudes towards the acceptance of change. Ask applicants how

they would react to particular examples of fast changing situations. What are their expectations of change? Have they experienced significant levels of change in past jobs and, if so, how did they cope? Are their general outlooks, perspectives and demeanours conducive to accommodating change?

Today, such attitudinal factors should be as crucial to the selection process as candidates' educational backgrounds and technical skills. A major tragedy (arguably *the* major tragedy) of British society over the last 30 years has been the enormous number of highly qualified workers (in the certificated sense) made unemployable because of the redundancy of their outdated skills – in conjunction with individual unwillingness to adopt new perspectives. One might have possessed armfuls of certificates and diplomas in various aspects of heavy engineering, shipbuilding, mining and other extraction, steelmaking, etc, but they counted for nothing when these industries finally collapsed.

Flexible workforces

Organisations increasingly employ labour on a part-time, casual, *ad hoc* and/or sub-contract basis.

Checkpoint

What proportions of your workforce (including managers) are (a) full time, (b) part time, (c) sub-contract labour? If all your employees are full time, how much would be saved if half of them were put on to part-time or casual contracts? If some employees already work in this manner, predict the economic effects of doubling the existing proportion of casual and part-time staff.

Three major factors explain the (massive) trend towards 'flexible' work in the United Kingdom.

1. Businesses often find that their permanent full-time employees are not fully occupied throughout the year (sometimes not even throughout an entire working week) so that contract labour hired for short periods and/or to undertake specific assignments is much cheaper than employing permanent staff.
2. The size of the firm's labour force can be varied at will.
3. Widespread redundancies and unprecedented high unemployment in the 1980s have released a large supply of workers willing – through choice or economic necessity – to work casually.

Clearly, new work patterns demand fresh approaches to labour management and the design of organisations. The common approach is to distinguish between 'core' and 'peripheral' workers. Core workers comprise full-time permanent employees who have security of tenure, receive training, and enjoy numerous fringe benefits. In return, however, their contracts of employment demand total job flexibility: they must stand ready to do whatever work is available, irrespective of occupational divisions, at any time. Core workers have no job description other than to complete any tasks that need doing.

Peripheral workers, conversely, are hired on short-term and/or part-time contracts whenever extra labour is required. They exercise little discretion over how they perform their work and (generally) do not have 'careers'. Peripheral staff may include job sharers, agency employees, self-employed consultants and sub-contract labour as well as casuals and part-timers; indeed, anyone who can be hired and fired quickly and easily as market conditions change may be categorised as a peripheral worker.

────────────────── *Checkpoint* ──────────────────

Apart from lower cost and greater convenience, how would you describe the advantages of a casual/part-time workforce? What are the disadvantages?

The *advantages* include the facts that:

(a) you need not be concerned about superannuation, promotion, annual pay rises or sick pay (other than the statutory minimum) for flexible workers;

(b) unions are often uninterested in having part-time or casual employees as members (regarding casuals as a threat to full-time jobs);

(c) unsatisfactory non-permanent workers may be easily discarded (few of them are covered by existing employment protection legislation).

There are, however, a number of *disadvantages*. Casually employed staff often lack commitment to their work, have (usually) received less training than full-time colleagues, and frequently resent being employed full time and/or under short-term contracts. Also, numerous frictions can arise from the employment of casual workers alongside permanent employees. Casual staff resent having to do the same work as full-time colleagues for lower pay and without equivalent conditions of service. Permanent workers, on the other hand, may regard casual employees as inferior and a danger to their security of employment, particularly where the overwhelming majority of casual workers are women and/or belong to an ethnic minority.

There are few opportunities for job enrichment in such circumstances; morale is usually low and rates of absenteeism and staff turnover are high. Even though casual workers are not normally unionised, industrial disputes still occur and, because they are not resolved through agreed management/union procedures, they are likely to be highly disruptive in the longer period. Grievances persist indefinitely in casual labour systems, transmitted from one generation of casual workers to the next without any possibility of resolution.

Adviceline

If the benefits of a flexible workforce exceed the cost, look carefully for ways of providing satisfying and meaningful work to peripheral employees. Networking (see Chapter 4), job sharing and formal career break systems can be especially helpful in this respect (though beware of the 'two Monday mornings' syndrome frequently attached to job-sharing arrangements). Such schemes:

(a) enhance the morale of flexible workers, who are made to feel wanted and of real value to the organisation;
(b) enable individuals to choose how and when they do their work;
(c) help employers of flexible labour to retain their best peripheral workers;
(d) help to overcome problems of low commitment, poor communication and shoddy work among casually employed staff.

Improving the performance of flexible employees

In order to manage a flexible workforce effectively you need separate policies for each of the following duties:

- appraising the calibre of peripheral workers (especially those who work off the premises);
- achieving the wholehearted participation of peripheral workers in the meetings, committees, etc, necessary for effective decision-taking within the business;
- preventing permanent employees from resenting 'special' treatment afforded to flexible staff (eg, if common grading and promotion systems apply to both core and peripheral workers);
- controlling the quality of recruitment of peripheral workers;
- securing loyalty among flexible workers;
- arranging for the supervision of peripheral employees and deciding whether this should be done by other peripherals in a higher grade or by core employees. Note that flexible workers are not usually capable of handling crises or sudden influxes of extra work since they lack the resources, information, experience and authority necessary for this. Bear in mind that this can lead to overwork among core staff.

Adviceline

Profit-sharing, holiday and sick pay and paid time off for the training of flexible workers are among the many strategies that may be employed to overcome some of these difficulties. Further devices include:

- paying peripheral workers to attend general discussions about the firm's objectives;
- making peripherals responsible for the quality of their output;
- offering fringe benefits (superannuation, for example) to peripherals;
- providing contractually binding guarantees of re-entry to jobs after a break in continuity of service;
- devising grievance and appeals procedures, consultation systems, etc, suitable for casually employed staff.

Induction of flexible workers into existing work groups is especially important, as it is essential that peripherals feel part of the team and are introduced to the wider aspects of the organisation.

Bonding the worker to the firm

How best can you create a sense of belonging among the company's employees? Single status (see Chapter 6) can be enormously helpful here, as can training, internal promotion and staff development, long-term job security and (most important) *symbols* of involvement with the enterprise.

If yours is a business that brings its employees into direct personal contact with customers, consider seriously the possibility of issuing uniforms to your workers. Not only will this help to bond the employee to the firm, but it will also enhance the image (see Chapter 5) of the company.

Staff uniforms

Today more UK workers wear company uniform than ever before. Nearly all the staff in franchised outlets are uniformed (as part of the general standardisation of premises, layout, product and working practices that franchising necessarily involves), as are the counter staff of several high street building societies and banks. In shops and department stores the wearing of uniform has been standard practice for generations. There are numerous advantages.

1. Staff receive a valuable fringe benefit; they no longer have to buy clothes for work.

117

2. Employees will always appear neat and tidy in front of customers. Management is saved the embarrassment of having to tell inappropriately or dirtily dressed workers to improve their clothing standards. If a person fails to wear or maintain the uniform properly (stained or torn garments, for example), the fact is both conspicuous and chastening to the individual concerned. Employees stand alongside identically uniformed fellow workers, so that a dirty uniform stands out in comparison with clean ones (much more than if people wear their own clothes).
3. Workers are encouraged to feel part and parcel of the organisation. The wearer of a staff uniform is identified without question as a member of the firm.
4. Staff uniforms create a basic equality within the workplace. This avoids problems connected with, for example, junior staff being expected not to 'outdress' their supervisors; or certain male employees being required to wear suits and ties and others only to wear casuals, or only the younger female staff being expected to wear short skirts, etc.
5. Since everyone wears the same clothes the only way individuals can compete with each other in relation to dress is for them to maintain their uniforms as immaculately as possible, hence stimulating employees' awareness of personal appearance.

Need for a positive image

The physical appearance of staff tells customers much about the character of the company: what it is; does; wishes to be and how it wants to relate to the outside environment. Appearances convey powerful non-verbal messages. Indeed, in many situations a staff uniform speaks to customers more loudly and clearly than most other forms of communication. The worker assumes the *personality* of the organisation. Accordingly, great care is needed when designing uniforms in order to ensure that appropriate images are transmitted. The message conveyed should be:

- positive;
- easy to read;
- modern (uniforms can quickly become outdated);
- honest, eloquent and helpful in providing useful information.

Problems with staff uniforms

Putting staff into uniform can greatly improve a company's outward concern for customer care. Consumers (it is hoped) will perceive the staff as dressing to please *customers* and not merely for their own benefit. The problem, of course, is that the solid, reliable and well-established company images that uniforms project may encourage among employees a conformist attitude and lack of initiative.

Having customer contact staff dress alike does not mean that you necessarily want them all to think and behave in the same manner. Conformity to standards may be desirable, but not to the extent that staff become unable (or unwilling) to do anything for themselves. Wearers of uniforms, moreover, sometimes adopt arrogant and officious attitudes towards outsiders – in keeping with their perceptions of the status of uniformed work. Several factors explain the latter phenomenon.

(a) How employees dress becomes totally determined by management which, in a sense, exercises a form of censorship over how the staff visually communicate with other people during working hours. Wearers of staff uniforms give up their *own* right to dress and be treated as individuals and may translate this into feelings that *others* need not be treated as individuals either – including the firm's customers.

(b) Uniforms may be mentally associated with rules and procedures, hence creating an organisational culture (see Chapter 8) inclined towards bureaucracy and red tape.

(c) Uniforms create anonymity. Thus, the uniformed employee can hide away behind the standardised modes of communication and behaviour that uniforms suggest psychologically.

(d) Staff may be encouraged to act mechanically, as if they were robots and little more than appendages to reception desks or shop counters.

Staff communications

A great many staff problems involve interpersonal and organisational communication difficulties. Effective internal communication, moreover, is crucial to management's ability to take correct decisions. To test your business's strengths and weaknesses in these respects ask yourself the following questions:

1. How long is it since you were last unsure of taking an important decision because you felt those around you were withholding crucial information? Do all the firm's employees know about its medium-term plans and policies for achieving its objectives? If not, why not?

2. How can you be sure that staff fully understand the communications transmitted to them by management? How can senior management be sure that it understands communications emanating from lower levels?

3. How frequently do senior staff suggest ideas for new strategies? If a strategy begins to fail, who will report the fact and what is the mechanism for implementing remedial action?

4. Consider the most successful activities your firm has undertaken during the last three years. How did the initial ideas for these arise? Did the original ideas seem impractical when they were proposed?

5. What were the most difficult aspects of the last three major decisions taken by your organisation? Would the provision of better information or better internal interpersonal relations have reduced these difficulties and, if so, why?

6. Think of the best and worst decisions the firm has taken over the last two years. What exactly caused these decisions to be good or bad?

7. Does the organisation have a mechanism for ensuring that relevant staff are up to date with new techniques and with the latest ideas in their specialist areas? If not, think up a system for achieving this objective (eg, internal distribution of technical literature, subscription to specialist magazines, interdepartmental exchange of technical information, etc).

8

How to Improve the Culture of Your Business

Introduction

A firm that devises sound and relevant strategies, which constantly seeks to improve the efficiency of its operations and which manages its workforce properly will find that a constructive, co-operative, enthusiastic and innovative atmosphere pervades the organisation. The atmosphere that exists within a firm may be termed its business 'culture'. Accordingly, this chapter will explain how a business culture arises, how it can be developed in appropriate directions and how and why it will affect the firm.

Checkpoint

Assuming that your definition of the company's mission (see Chapter 1) is clear and adequate, how many of the firm's junior, middle and senior employees do you think are genuinely committed to achieving the company's objectives? If the answer is 'not many', why is this the case?

Can you devise incentive schemes which generate personal benefits to those who openly and wholeheartedly commit themselves to the organisation's common purpose?

Adviceline

Conspicuously encourage employees who overtly display their loyalty to the business. This will stimulate enterprise and effort and provide a good example to other workers. Reward allegiance through declarations of approval and possibly with higher wages. I remember a junior employee of a leading UK motor distributor who took the initiative and arranged a company dinner-dance; she organised the event, sold the tickets, booked the hotel, hired and paid the band, etc. The occasion was a huge success which greatly enhanced the firm's image. Yet the employee received no thanks from the company's management - not even an acknowledgement of the value of her contribution. A formal 'thank you', accompanied perhaps by a small gift, would simultaneously have impelled the employee to further endeavours on behalf of the company and presented a splendid example to other staff members.

Common perspectives

In a well-managed firm, employees at all levels of authority will share common perspectives about the factors that determine its prosperity and future prospects. Such perspectives concern the guiding principles that govern the firm's work; how things should be done, when, by whom, and how enthusiastically.

To some extent these perceptions may be created by management via its internal communications, style of leadership, organisation system and working methods; but they can only be sustained and brought to bear on day-to-day operations by the firm's workers. Staff should *feel* they possess a common objective. They need to experience a sense of affinity with the organisation and *want* to pursue a common cause.

The existence of common perspectives helps employees to interpret day-to-day events and to structure and reinforce their views about the company.

--------------------------------- *Checkpoint* ---------------------------------

How do you think workers see the motives that drive the firm? Are these motives perceived as, for example:

- making profits for the company's owners;
- satisfying consumer needs;
- providing employment for workers;
- serving the community;
- some other consideration (specify)?

Which of these employee perceptions do you regard as desirable and which undesirable?

Determinants of common perspectives

Individuals enter a business from differing cultural backgrounds and environments. Within the firm, however, employees must interact with colleagues who possibly hold widely disparate attitudes, perceptions and opinions. Accordingly, certain measures are needed to encourage common perspectives and to bind workers to the firm. The following factors contribute to the formation of common perspectives:

- Frequent personal contacts between senior and junior employees, especially if important company matters are dealt with at these interactions (fetching a senior manager a cup of tea does not qualify as a serious point of contact).

- Employees' awareness of the extent and severity of the external competition confronting the business, plus a recognition that workers' jobs depend on the company's competitive success. People who see their livelihoods threatened by a hostile external environment are likely to perceive the organisation as protecting personal welfare against a dangerous outside world.
- Feelings among employees that they belong to a highly selective group.

Adviceline

Staff recruitment procedures (interviewing, selection tests, etc) are themselves useful devices for impressing job applicants with the prestige of the company. The successful candidate's image of the firm, its culture and employee values will derive to some extent from how he or she is treated during the selection process.

Recruits are more likely to be loyal to the organisation if they regard membership of it as somehow special and exclusive to only the very best people. Appointed applicants then experience a sense of achievement in having been admitted, which greatly contributes to morale and team spirit within their eventual working groups.

- Employees with similar backgrounds, ages, general outlook, educational experience, etc, are frequently like-minded and thus more likely to adopt common perspectives.
- Satisfactory employee attitudes are more likely if employees' work is varied, interesting and directly and obviously relevant to the attainment of common objectives.

Every employee should know why the firm exists, what it does, its history and outline structure. Equally, staff have to be made aware of the need for high quality output, for good interpersonal relations, maximum operational efficiency, and for total commitment to customer care.

Resistance to change

As common perspectives emerge, individuals start to behave as they feel other employees *expect* them to behave. They begin to work as a team, co-operating and co-ordinating their efforts to achieve common goals.

Unfortunately, dangers as well as benefits surround the development of common perspectives; existing perceptions may become so integrated into employees' attitudes that they become set in their ways and extremely resistant to change. Staff come to believe that the company's views and actions are always right, regardless of circumstances. No deviations from standard practices are allowed.

――――――――――――― *Checkpoint* ―――――――――――――

To what extent do your senior colleagues always conform to the organisational status quo? Do they adhere to fixed routines and expect others to follow? How adequately do they accommodate new working methods?

Adviceline

Resistance to change is arguably the most serious problem confronting organisations. It can be avoided more readily if:

- details of changes in the firm's objectives are instantly communicated to all workers;
- expectations of company and individual performances are regularly reviewed (via appraisal and/or management by objectives interviews, for example);
- employees have a wide range of contacts in other departments;
- there is frequent job rotation;
- remuneration systems are linked to the introduction of new products and working methods;
- individual employees have little to lose following a rearrangement of working practices;
- junior staff are free to express their ideas.

Organisational culture

An organisation's culture determines employees' perceptions, values and norms of behaviour. It consists of customary ways of doing things and of employees' feelings about issues that affect the firm. Cultures evolve gradually; indeed, employees may not even be aware that a culture exists. Nevertheless, cultures are important because they help to define how workers see and feel about each other, their jobs, and their relations with the business.

――――――――――――― *Checkpoint* ―――――――――――――

Prepare a list of at least ten words or phrases that accurately sum up the culture of your organisation. If you find this easy you have probably misunderstood the issue – the exercise is much more difficult than it first appears. The list might include such words as: paternalistic, easy-going, risk-averse, autocratic, etc.

Effects of culture

In 1916 Henri Fayol, a French mining engineer, published a book, *General and Industrial Management*, suggesting the existence of five basic functions of management: planning and forecasting, organisation, co-ordination, command and control. This categorisation is as useful today as when it first appeared; it is extremely difficult to devise a better and more comprehensive definition of what management is all about.

Consider, therefore, the effects of an organisation's culture on each of these functions.

1. *Planning and forecasting*

   This means looking into the future and deciding what to do in the future, assuming the occurrence of various events. The firm's culture determines who prepares its plans (a small group of top managers or a more representative collection of people drawn from all its sections, departments, subsidiaries and divisions); whether plans are imposed arbitrarily or offered for discussion; and the degree of centralisation or decentralisation in decision making and the implementation of programmes.

Checkpoint

How are plans determined in your organisation: autocratically or with employee participation? Have you considered alternative methods?

Adviceline

Participative planning is usually the best:

- it ensures that ridiculously high and impracticable targets are not set, because those who would have to achieve them are involved in the determination of objectives;
- the skills, experience and detailed knowledge of operations possessed by lower ranking employees are incorporated into the planning process;
- less experienced staff receive training in planning methods;
- employee morale should improve as participants come to influence the events that affect their working lives;
- staff are (usually) more willing to implement plans that they helped to create.

---

2. *Organisation*

   Culture helps to determine the formality of company rules and procedures, the rigidity of systems (conventional line and staff versus more flexible structures), authority and accountability arrangements, interpersonal relations between various grades of employees, etc. All these matters should be *consciously regulated* (see Chapter 4).

3. *Co-ordination*
See Chapter 3 for information on co-ordination techniques. The main options are to have either a strong centralised system or *ad hoc* and/or temporary methods.

4. *Command*
Leadership style (see Chapter 6) may be authoritarian or democratic, permissive or directive, tight or flexible, according to the firm's managerial culture.

Checkpoint

How closely do your company's managers supervise their subordinates? Do they issue precise and detailed instructions, or specify broad overall objectives leaving workers to achieve these as they please? Has your firm established a policy regarding leadership style?

Adviceline

Deciding which style of command to adopt is difficult because so much depends on the circumstances of particular situations. Allowing employees to choose how they complete assignments can make work more interesting and improve job satisfaction. However, not everyone responds positively to the democratic approach, particularly where:

- the work undertaken is innately uninteresting;
- there is scope for disagreement about which working methods are most effective for completing employees' tasks;
- lack of positive direction could prevent the attainment of objectives;
- quick and/or unpopular decisions are necessary.

Recognise and accept that some people prefer being told what to do rather than being consulted and having to participate in taking decisions.

Ultimately, the only way to assess the effectiveness of a leadership style is to examine its consequences for productivity. If (substantial) targets are always met without a high long-term staff turnover rate or frequent requests for interdepartmental transfers, it is reasonable to conclude that the firm's current leadership style is satisfactory. These matters are discussed fully in Chapter 6.

5. *Control*

Control means setting targets, monitoring activities, comparing actual performance with targets and then taking action to remedy deficiencies. Culture affects control through determining the nature of the firm's monitoring and appraisal systems (eg, whether performance appraisal is to be part of the firm's disciplinary rather than counselling procedures) and through establishing the consequences of poor performance.

Adviceline

The purpose of appraisal must always be to *improve performance* and *not* to discipline the worker. A good system will investigate not only the appraisee's personal strengths and weaknesses but also the barriers that management may have created which prevent the employee achieving his or her goals, eg, lack of resources, communications breakdowns, failure of senior management to delegate enough authority to the employee, and so on.

Organisational cultures in practice

Cultures do not just happen; they result from management initiatives, from the behaviour and attitudes of workers, and from a wide variety of environmental factors.

Certain companies (mostly in the United States) publish details of their desired corporate cultures. Here are some examples.

US electronic measurement company

We believe in open and frank communications, consultative management style, concern for the individual and respect for his or her judgement. We emphasise the need to assume risk and to create an entrepreneurial climate. A high value is placed on innovative, creative results. We respect different viewpoints, and will tolerate and understand occasional failures. Full commitment to agreed goals is expected, as are the highest standards of personal and business ethics and of positive, inspirational leadership.

US computer equipment company

We believe that employees are honest and trustworthy and should be treated with dignity and respect. We assume that our employees want to achieve their full potential and will work hard to do so. Employees want to understand the purpose of their work and the goals of the organisation. They want to be held accountable for results and to be recognised and rewarded for achievements.

US finance corporation

The company is committed to helping talented and able people to develop their skills and assume greater responsibility. We shall make certain that ideas, concerns and problems are identified and that two-way communication is effectively maintained. Our aim is to provide an environment that identifies, encourages and rewards excellence, innovation and high quality customer service.

Multinational motor car manufacturer

Our success is directly attributable to a strong set of central values shared by our employees across the globe. These include:

- a strong commitment to innovation;
- a passion for excellence;
- integrity, honesty and respect for individuals;
- individual initiative and decision-taking at the decentralised level;
- an open style and informality in communications.

US automotive company

Fundamental to our success are these basic values:

- employee involvement and teamwork;
- total commitment to customer service;
- quest for profit;
- quality comes first;
- continuous improvement of products;
- dealers and suppliers are our partners.

US computer manufacturer

The core values of this corporation are:

(1) respect for the individual;
(2) giving the customer the best possible service;
(3) pursuit of excellence and superior performance.

The above are but snippets taken from quite extensive statements (some running to two or three pages) of intended corporate cultures. Nevertheless, the examples quoted should have given you the broad idea.

Note how these statements are generally worded, but focus mainly on customer care, on a relaxed management style (see Chapter 6) and respect for individual values. Of these, customer care is undoubtedly the most important. Genuine concern for customers necessarily causes the organisation to analyse its markets and to become highly sensitive to environmental change.

--------------------------------- *Checkpoint* ---------------------------------

What do you understand by the term 'customer care'? Read the next
section and then review your definition.

Customer care

Customer care is far more than after-sales service, although the latter
is an essential part of your company's total customer service effort.
Without customers the business would not exist, so a procedure for
creating satisfaction among the people who actually purchase your
products is just as essential for the firm's survival as efficient production
lines or marketing systems. Satisfied customers repeat their purchases
and introduce new consumers to the company. Note, moreover, that it
is much cheaper to obtain a repeat order than an order from a
completely new customer, since no additional advertising or other
selling effort is involved. Thus, it is nothing more than sound business
sense to become wholeheartedly committed to customer care.

Improving customer care

To be excellent at customer care, employees need to be able to perceive
the firm's operations *from the customer's viewpoint*. Regularly circulate to
your employees information about customers' responses to the company's activities, and be especially concerned to tell production staff of
successes achieved in the marketing area.

Remind office workers that the letters they write, the way they
answer the telephone, their appearance to outsiders who visit the firm,
etc, all directly contribute to customer relations. Shabby external
images (caused, for example, by badly worded or shoddily word
processed letters) can sabotage the customer care efforts of factory
floor production operatives.

A customer care programme needs to begin with a comprehensive
audit of all the company's customer care activities, including:

- the availability of spare parts and servicing facilities;
- the length of product guarantees compared to those offered by
  competitors;
- the clarity of instruction manuals;
- the availability of post-purchase advice on use of the product;
- the efforts to maintain contact with the customer via mailshots,
  newsletters, etc, in order to inform existing customers of new
  models, product improvements, and so on;
- the accuracy and appearance of documents sent to the customer
  (invoices, for example);
- the convenience of product packaging;

- the speed with which the firm handles customer queries and/or complaints;
- the lead time between the customer placing an order and delivery of the goods;
- the reliability of quoted delivery dates;
- the ease with which customers can place orders;
- the extent to which customers are consulted prior to modifying products;
- the extent to which information is given about ingredients, product uses, etc;
- the courtesy of company representatives;
- the availability of emergency help to customers;
- the convenience to customers of the systems through which they pay for their purchases.

Adviceline

Induction procedures for new employees are crucial for indoctrinating freshly recruited staff in the culture of the enterprise. Impressions gained by new employees during induction programmes can remain with them for long periods. Be prepared, therefore, to spend time and resources on induction systems. In particular:

- every new employee (no matter how junior the capacity in which that person is to be employed) should be welcomed personally by a *senior* member of staff;
- heads of department, supervisors, etc, should be instructed to spend time with the recruit and genuinely try to be helpful;
- the firm's organisational structure should be explained to the new entrant, together with that person's place within it and the importance of his or her contribution to the prosperity of the business.

The company's mission must be outlined and directly related to the recruit's specific duties. Efficiency and quality standards should be detailed, plus information about what the new entrant should do if he or she experiences problems, eg, if the recruit has difficulties with the work or does not get along with colleagues.

Revitalising apathetic workers

Organisational cultures can move in various directions, some of which are better than others. The ideal culture is one that generates:

- awareness of the need for change in the company's operations;

- willingness to collaborate with other departments and colleagues;
- acceptance of challenging targets;
- innovative attitudes and a desire to achieve results.

Some businesses consciously seek to manipulate their worker's cultural orientations, usually in an attempt to revitalise apathetic employees. They may do this through:

- encouraging intense competition for promotion;
- stimulating entrepreneurial attitudes among department heads (eg, by making them personally responsible for budgets, for hiring and firing staff, etc);
- placing great emphasis on success and achievement while openly denigrating employees who fail;
- giving top priority (perhaps mistakenly) to marketing rather than production skills;
- hiring and rapidly promoting younger people who possess certain business and technical qualifications;
- deliberately creating 'perpetual creative tension' in order to motivate employees (eg, by regularly increasing departmental output and profit requirements);
- rewarding top performers highly while paying others an extremely low wage.

Adviceline

People are sometimes paid according to past achievements rather than their current contributions to the business. They were promoted and rewarded on the basis of previously acquired (and currently outdated) qualifications, skills and experiences. Today, their worth to the company is lower than it was in the past; yet they continue to receive a high salary.

There is no easy way of dealing with this problem. The options include:

- finding the employee other things to do (although, unfortunately, he or she may not be capable of satisfactorily completing alternative duties);
- 'red-circling' an older employee, ie continuing to pay a wage higher than his or her objective worth, but insisting that the next person to do the job will be employed in a lower grade at a reduced salary;
- redundancy of the employee.

The problem with red-circling is that it can create enormous resentments among the employees who succeed overpaid people. Replacements may feel that they have been unfairly discriminated

---

against and that they too deserve the previous incumbent's high wage. People have even complained to industrial tribunals about this practice.

Redundancy could be the fairest solution to all concerned. In law 'redundancy' means that the business no longer has any work for the employee to perform. The redundancy concept is quite independent of the personality of the worker involved: it is the *job* that becomes redundant rather than the particular employee – who then ceases to be employed, circumstantially, because he or she happens to be the last incumbent of the position.

You are required by law to seek alternative work for anyone threatened with redundancy and – if he or she has been continuously employed for at least two years – to pay a limited amount of compensation (see Chapter 9 of my book, *Personal Effectiveness*, published by Kogan Page, 1988).

The outright dismissal of the employee in these circumstances would only be 'fair' in the legal sense (and hence not involve your losing a case in an industrial tribunal) if you can *prove* his or her inadequate performance, with evidence, witnesses, documented details of specific personal deficiencies, etc. You are legally obliged to give the employee written warnings of alleged inadequacies and to offer the person an opportunity to improve his or her standards, possibly accompanied by additional training.

Changing an existing culture

Unsatisfactory cultures can become so deeply embedded within the infrastructure of an organisation that they cannot be removed easily (local authority offices, the Civil Service and universities and technical colleges are examples that immediately spring to mind). In commercial organisations, stark and perhaps unpleasant decisions may be necessary in these circumstances, including perhaps:

- drastic redundancy and redeployment programmes, replacing or reallocating to other duties perhaps as much as 80 per cent of current workers;
- conspicuously recruiting younger, better qualified and more energetic people on salaries far higher than those paid to existing workers, and making it abundantly clear that the high wages reflect the entrants' vigour, flexibility and ability to cope with change;
- extensive use of outside agencies, consultants and sub-contractors to undertake work previously completed in house;
- forming a small 'crisis management' team of key personnel with draconian powers to overturn departmental decisions, establish

cost centres, determine budgets and demand explanations from *any* member of staff;
- hiring external business turnaround specialists on .short-term contracts with the brief to revitalise the organisation (payments by results is normally the best way to remunerate these outsiders).

Otherwise you will simply have to admit defeat and change the company's strategies to satisfy cultural constraints, usually by reducing targets and expectations.

Role of senior management

Effective 'culture control' by a company's management requires that the following rules are followed.

(a) Management must openly demonstrate its own commitment to the culture it is attempting to develop.
(b) Warning signals attached to employees' declining commitment (apathy, lethargy, failure to attend meetings, etc) must be dealt with immediately they occur.

Adviceline

Act instantly and, where necessary, drastically to counteract outward manifestations of bad attitude (eg, employees making abusive comments about the firm, loss of enthusiasm, bad time-keeping, absenteeism, etc). Redeploy staff, rearrange workloads, change working practices, conduct disciplinary interviews, and so on. But, above all, *communicate* with these workers. Find the causes of adverse perceptions and what you can do to remedy grievances.

(c) The company's general expertise and areas of special competence (research, introduction of completely new products, customer service, etc) should be broadcast to all workers. Give your employees lots of information about company operations; let them be proud of working for the business.
(d) Management must recognise that employee commitment to the company's mission will only occur if the firm's purpose coincides with workers' self-interest. This could mean having to relate each person's remuneration to his or her contribution to attaining company objectives. Note how the salary structure emerging from such a system may not correspond to that currently operating within the firm.

---------------------- *Checkpoint* ----------------------

Does the highest paid person in your business contribute most to achieving its mission? Does the second highest paid employee make the second greatest contribution, the third highest paid the third most important contribution, and so on. If not, why not?

CHECKLIST

1. Is the culture of your organisation fully compatible with its mission, its strategies and working methods? If not, why not and what must be done to improve shortcomings?
2. Describe your perception of employees' current attitudes towards:
   - productivity
   - quality of output
   - the firm's public image
   - the importance of customers.
3. How easily could your company's core values be altered? If the answer is 'not easily at all', why is this the case?
4. Do employees dress smartly for work, even if they do not come into contact with outsiders and are not instructed to dress in a certain manner?

Adviceline

Employees who bother to dress well to come to work subconsciously demonstrate their satisfaction with the company and with their jobs. They are saying that they regard the work experience and how they are seen by colleagues as an important aspect of their lives. Conversely, people who do not wash themselves properly, or who wear dirty and unironed clothes for work, transmit dramatic messages about how they perceive the company.

---

5. Are departmental managers excessively concerned with their prestige and personal status in comparison with other departmental managers? If so, how important are the firm's status differentials relative to its capacity to achieve its objectives?
6. When employees discuss their colleagues do they normally describe them favourably? If people constantly criticise their fellow-workers, what does this tell you about the culture of the business?
7. What is the attitude of both senior and junior staff towards working long hours, taking work home, pressure of deadlines, etc?

Adviceline

Willingness to work long hours is an excellent barometer of how employees feel about their jobs.

---

8. Do employees *ask* to be sent on training courses? Are they keen to acquire additional qualifications, experiences and skills that might benefit the company more than themselves?
9. If the firm subscribes to technical and professional journals, the financial press and specialist trade magazines, how avidly are these read by the employees to whom they are circulated? Indicators of this are (a) whether employees comment on things they have seen and read in these publications, (b) how long it takes for a magazine to go through the distribution list, and (c) whether employees begin to use up-to-date technical jargon picked up from these journals.
10. Do you think employees regard the organisation as supporting rather than interfering with their work?

Adviceline

The best way to find this out is to ask employees for their views. Do this during appraisal interviews.

Other questions to ask are whether employees regard the firm's organisation structure (see Chapter 4) as rigid or flexible, whether in their opinion the organisation is resistant to change, and whether they understand the goals of the departments in which they work. Further issues to explore are:

- the extent to which employees' jobs provide opportunities for self-development;
- whether other people are seen as helping or hindering a particular individual's efforts;
- employees' perceptions of management's style of leadership (see Chapter 6);
- whether individuals can easily approach senior managers with work-related problems.

Further Reading

Kogan Page publish a wide range of books for business. A list is available on application to 120 Pentonville Road, London N1 9JN.

Index